S R NATHAN

50 stories
from my life

The publisher would like to acknowledge the following for their contributions:

S R Nathan Education Upliftment Fund
Cover photo by E K Yap, courtesy of *Singapore Tatler*

First published in 2013 by
Editions Didier Millet Pte Ltd
35B Boat Quay Singapore 049824
www.edmbooks.com

Text © S R Nathan 2013
Illustrations © Morgan Chua 2013

Reprinted 2013, 2014, 2016 (twice)

Printed in Singapore by NPE Print Communications Pte Ltd

ISBN: 978-981-4385-34-3

S R NATHAN

50 stories
from my life

S R Nathan

with
Timothy Auger

Illustrations by
Morgan Chua

edm EDITIONS DIDIER MILLET

CONTENTS

*Dedicated with love to my wife, Umi, who has devoted herself
to providing me with the companionship, support and encouragement
I needed to walk the unexpected journey of my life.*

ACKNOWLEDGEMENTS

My memoirs, *Path to the Presidency: An Unexpected Journey*, recorded a lifetime of experiences – tragedy, deprivation, struggles as a runaway. At a time when I was resigned to my fate, the Second World War changed my life. I discovered my own potential, and strove thereafter to live my life as successfully as I could. Thus began my journey of progress.

I felt that the full version of my memoirs might be difficult for young readers to read and absorb. Hence the idea of '50 Stories from My Life' – shorter and more readable, and accompanied by caricatures. Where possible, I have tried to draw some lessons, which I hope my young readers may find useful in their own lives.

I want to record my thanks to Timothy Auger who authored my original memoirs together with me. The task of picking these stories out of the full version of my memoirs and re-telling them in this simpler form was his contribution to the production of this book. To Associate Professor Ang Cheng Guan, my former colleague from my days in the Institute of Defence and Strategic Studies (IDSS), I owe a special thanks for reading through the drafts of each of the 50 stories and giving me and Tim valuable advice from his experience as a teacher/educator. My grateful thanks are due to Professor Arnoud de Meyer, President of the Singapore Management University, who also read the stories and drew out of them lessons that appear both in the Contents list and woven into the narrative. To him I owe a special debt.

Last but not least, I thank Bobby Chin, Chairman of my 'Upliftment Fund' for authorising support for the cost of the production of this book; and I must say a heartfelt 'thank you' to my dear friend Didier Millet for pushing me to believe that rendering my memoirs in this form was possible for the benefit of readers of school age.

I hope young people will enjoy reading this book, and find in it some lessons to think about.

S R Nathan

INTRODUCTION

5*0 Stories from My Life* recalls a number of key episodes in the personal and official life of one of Singapore's most distinguished public servants.

The end of Mr Nathan's second term of office as President of Singapore, at the end of August 2011, was followed by the publication of his memoirs, *An Unexpected Journey: Path to the Presidency*. The book received great acclaim from both expert reviewers and the general public.

This new publication will bring some of the highlights from Mr Nathan's life to a more general audience, and particularly to younger readers. Mr Nathan lived through childhood poverty and family tragedy; learning to be self-reliant, he survived the Japanese occupation; he acquired further education in adult life; rose from the bottom to a senior rank in the civil service; worked overseas as a diplomat; ran a newspaper group; and became Singapore's elected president.

Over nearly nine decades, Mr Nathan has learned many lessons from personal experience. Some of his recollections and insights are brought together in this book, in the hope that they may be useful to later generations, and give a better understanding of how Singapore came to be the Singapore we know.

THE JOYS OF CHILDHOOD

My early childhood was very happy, and left me with many good memories. I was fortunate to have loving parents. Later in life, I never forgot how much I owed to them. I also learned that good times do not always last, and therefore one must learn to value them.

I was born in Singapore on 3 July 1924. When I was very young, because of problems connected with my father's work, we moved to Muar, a small port town on the west coast of Johor, the southernmost state in the Malay peninsula.

At that time, what we now call 'Malaysia' did not yet exist. The British oversaw the government of Malaya, including Johor. It was only after World War II that the peninsular Malay states came together to form the Federation of Malaya, which became independent in 1957.

Our home overlooked the Muar River. Our house was one of a row of shophouses, with a five-foot way, set back from the river bank. The building is still there, although its appearance has changed quite a bit. The ships that plied between

Muar and Singapore would come over the horizon and sail past us on their way to the dock. Every time one appeared, my sisters and I would rush to an upstairs window and watch – the ships seemed to grow bigger and bigger as they approached.

We also watched the comings and goings of the Muar ferry. In those days the ferry was the only way people and their vehicles travelling between Johor Bahru and Malacca could cross the river. There was no bridge. Cars and lorries drove up planks to board the craft. When it was fully loaded, a wooden pole was placed across the end. The ferry was then pushed away from the bank, and a motor launch would haul it across to the other side.

Several of the shophouses were occupied by firms of lawyers. My father, whose name was Sellapan, was a lawyer's clerk. Besides my mother, Abhirami, the family consisted of two older sisters, Paruvatham and Amurtham, and me, Ramanathan.

I did have another sister, Sivayogam, the eldest. However, there is a tradition among Tamils that, if the omens are not favourable when a child is born – for example, if the horoscope and the time of birth are not satisfactory – the parents give him or her away. The baby is taken to the temple and the priest carries out a ceremony. The child is 'handed over to God'. In this way my mother gave away my eldest sister. She was to be cared for by my aunt (my mother's sister), whose name was Pakiam.

The ferry taking cars across the Muar River.

My sister and I enjoyed watching the ships come and go on the Muar River.

It was a happy time. My father was doing well in his job. We lived comfortably with the occasional little luxury. Sometimes we enjoyed British biscuits and other goodies. Some of my toys were ordered from Robinson's in Singapore, the famous department store, which occupied a big building in Raffles Place. I had a wooden rocking horse. Once I cut off its tail, thinking it would grow again. We played football in a field near the house – my sisters used to wear normal shoes tied round with string to make them look like proper football boots.

When I was around six years old, I went to a nearby primary school, run by a Tamil schoolmaster. It was in a small bungalow, near the courthouse. All I can remember about my lessons is the excitement of learning my ABC. The class was quite small – about ten. At school, I met other children and enjoyed myself. One of my sisters was in a school nearby, so the whole experience was fun.

At home we spoke Tamil. In my father's office, he and his colleagues spoke only English, and I myself started to pick up some English at school.

My father's family, originally from southern India, had been in Singapore for two generations. He was quite athletic, and used to play for a Malay football team in Singapore. My mother dressed in the Malay style. In fact, in our daily lives, we did not identify ourselves particularly with India. We were very localised.

The Muar River, seen from the town.

We did go to the Hindu temple in Muar. Sometimes there were festivals. We would watch the silver chariot pass in front of the house, and we loved the fireworks. The temple events were organised by the Chettiars, Indian merchants specialising in money-lending and banking. My grandmother on my mother's side had married a Chettiar, so my mother had links to their community.

One of the earliest events I can remember is going off to school in Singapore. My father took me there by taxi, together with my sisters, so that they could all attend the wedding of one of my cousins. My only recollection of the journey is my first sight of Newton Circus, in those days just a roundabout. Flyovers were a thing of the future. My father and sisters returned to Muar, and in the weeks that followed, I missed my family dreadfully.

Many of the clients of my father's firm were rubber planters and smallholders, and they were badly affected by the slump that hit the rubber industry in the 1930s. The firm's income dropped. Because of stress, my father developed a drinking problem, and ran up debts. Before long the whole family was evicted from our home by the Chettiar moneylenders. They had to leave Muar in a hurry and join me across the Causeway in Singapore. For my family, the happy days had come to an end. I learned that good times could not be taken for granted. Good times can unexpectedly change for the worse, for reason's beyond one's control.

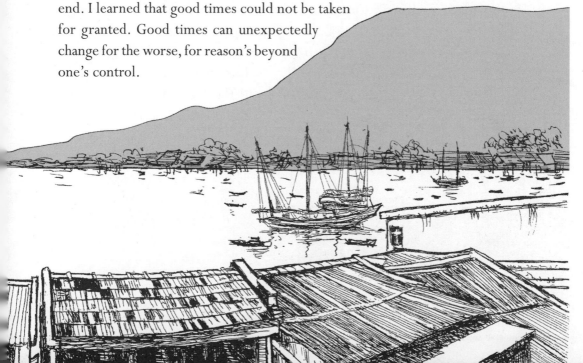

TOUGH LESSONS FOR A YOUNG BOY

When I was still very young, I was sent away from Muar to school in Singapore. There I learned that life is not always fair. What matters is the way we face the challenges we meet. Children often do things with disastrous consequences. In dealing with them, adults must practise what they preach.

For a while, I lived with the family of one of my uncles, in Hooper Road. I entered the Anglo-Chinese Primary School, in Standard One, and soon moved up to Standard Two. The school stood where the National Archives building is today. We had fun climbing the steep slope of Fort Canning Hill, until one boy suffered a tragic fall. Every day I travelled to school on the trolley-buses. These were electric buses, picking up their power from overhead cables, rather like trams.

I enjoyed my lessons. The school was run by Methodists. Methodism is a form of Protestantism, part of the Christian tradition. Although I was Hindu, I went to chapel with all the other children. My mother said, 'God is the same whoever you are …'. This was still the time of British colonial rule, and we had to sing the British national anthem, 'God Save the King'. Because King George V had a beard, we used to sing 'God Shave the King' instead!

We sang the British national anthem, changing the words to 'God Shave the King'.

A few months after I came to Singapore, I was joined by my parents and sisters. I was overjoyed to see them again, but behind their move lay a sad story. In Muar, my father had run up debts with the Chettiars, which he couldn't repay. My family was thrown out of their house and had to leave. So they also came to live in my uncle's house.

After we had all been together at Hooper Road for a month or so, my parents sensed that my uncle and his family did not want us to stay. Perhaps the house was too crowded. We were then taken in for a while by my aunt Pakiam, my mother's elder sister, after which we moved to a little attap house in what is now Rambutan Road.

My father tried desperately to find a job. Because of a slump in the rubber plantation business, there were few vacancies in lawyers' offices. Finally he began working for a granite-quarrying company in Changi. It was not a happy time for him. Perhaps because of stress created by his debts, perhaps because of difficulties in finding work, my father had taken to drinking too much alcohol, often wasting most of his wages. One Sunday he brought home some fresh crabs, and we had a wonderful lunch. However, later that day, tragedy struck. In the evening, after my father had returned to the quarry, we received a message from the police. He had committed suicide. My world fell apart.

The next day I was going to school on the bus. When I was about to pay the fare, an Eurasian neighbour told me to put my money away, and paid for my ticket. She must have heard what had happened. I was too young to know how to thank her, but that small act of kindness has stayed in my memory ever since.

My aunt Pakiam also showed great kindness, taking us back into her house in Ceylon Road. It was quite small, built of wood, and had an attap roof. At the back there was a large wooden platform used for storage, and there we squatted on the wooden floor and ate our food. Cooking was done over a wood fire. We ate mostly Indian food – vegetables, a bit of fish, on special occasions a chicken. We couldn't have imagined the quality of food available to Singaporeans today. There was no electricity. At night a kerosene lamp gave me just enough light to do my homework and study for exams. Life was simple.

Meanwhile I progressed well at school as a 'free' student, exempt from paying fees. I reached Standard Five. At that time many boys followed boxing, collecting pictures of champions and pasting them into exercise books. My enthusiasm led me into trouble. To increase my collection, I foolishly bought newspaper cuttings from my classmates on account. My debts mounted, and I could not pay them. When a couple of boys threatened me, I tried to get my own back by taking two of their schoolbooks, selling them, and paying them back. They reported me, and without any questions being asked I was expelled from the school. I was in the wrong, but I felt then, and I still feel, that the principal did not show much of the compassion his religious teaching required.

Now aged 12, I was sent away again to live with my relatives, who had moved from Hooper Road to Race Course Road. My cousin got me into the Rangoon Road Afternoon School. I did well, and transferred to the Victoria Afternoon School at Standard VII-A, and then to

Aunt Pakiam had an attap house in Ceylon Road.

the morning school. I failed the first time in my Standard VII exam, largely because I did not have several textbooks and could not cope.

Then, once again, disaster came. One day, while we were watching a cricket match at the Victoria School field from the school verandah, one of my schoolmates lost some books. Because I had been standing near the classroom I was accused of stealing them. 'All the evidence points to you,' said a teacher. 'If you don't own up I will send you to the police.' I protested my innocence. The school principal gave me a caning on the hand, and I was sacked from the school.

Despite my innocence, I could not face hurting my mother for a second time. I thought hard. In desperation, I came to a decision that would affect the future course of my life. I would run away from home.

CHAPTER 3

LIFE AS A RUNAWAY

At the age of 16, having been thrown out of school for the second time,
I ran away, and ended up in Muar, my childhood home and
the only place I knew outside Singapore. It was a rash thing to do,
but as a result I began to learn about life the hard way. I learned also
that kindness can come from unexpected directions.

Making some excuse to my mother, I grabbed a bottle of coffee, put a couple of books in my schoolbag and left home. First I went to the Theatre Royal, where they showed Tamil films. After the end of the show, I hid in a dark corner and spent the night there, using my books as a pillow. For about a week I slept rough in the streets, finding secluded spots around Arab Street and North Bridge Road. In those days it was common to see people sleeping in the five-foot ways, many of them workers in coffee-shops and other businesses nearby. After 10.00 pm the streets were very quiet. I had to beg for food. Some days I got lucky, other days I did not.

Gradually moving further and further away from Katong, I ended up at the Tanjong Pagar docks, where there was no security and anyone could go in and out. There was a food shelter for Indian workers. I queued up hopefully, but was turned away – 'Workers only!'

A bystander saw what was happening, and in an act of kindness shared his lunch with me. I was exhausted and hadn't washed properly for days – he took me to the house where he lived in a makeshift cubicle, gave me some soap and water, and lent me a *sarong* while I washed my clothes. I slept solidly for a day and a night. I asked if I could stay there. He tried to persuade me to go home, but finally agreed.

A week or two later Pavadai, as he was called, got me a job as an office boy with an architect's firm in the Union Building, on Collyer Quay. I worked there for a couple of months, but I was afraid that while running errands I might

bump into one of my brothers-in-law. They also worked in the area. Although I was desperate to see my mother and my siblings, I did not want to hurt them anymore. I was determined not to return until I had achieved something in life.

I decided to go back to Muar in Johor, which I remembered from my childhood. There was an overnight Straits Steamship service from Clifford Pier that I had used with my parents. I discovered that for ten cents you could get a *sampan* to take you out to the ship. On board you could have a word with the most senior Malay or Chinese deck hand, and for a dollar you could use his bunk. This was a strictly unofficial arrangement – there were proper passenger facilities.

With nine dollars in my pocket I arrived at Muar. I remembered our family barber, Mr Alagoo, and went to find him. He and his wife took me in for a while. To make ends meet I offered tuition for a dollar or so a month, but did not make much. For a time I worked delivering documents for a Chinese petition-

After dark, the five-foot ways were very quiet.

writer, who wrote letters and other important documents in English for people who could not speak or write the language.

Then I met an Indian muslim called Kader. He was a hawker selling food in the Malay school. I became his assistant, and went to live in his kampong, where I stayed for a couple of years. I called him 'Nana', Tamil for 'uncle'.

In search of a job I went to the lawyer's office where my father had worked, and above which we had lived. The chief clerk and his colleagues remembered me, and they were friendly enough, but they could not help. I got an appointment with the owner's son, who could hardly be bothered to take his eyes off the document he was reading while telling me there was no job.

My morale was low. Nana did his best to encourage me with stories about a Sufi saint from Nagore, India, and his miracles. I had a friend in the kampong, Noordin, who used to talk about Islam — I think he was slowly trying to get me to embrace his religion.

For a long time I had no contact with my family in Singapore. One day I asked Nana to visit my mother and bring back some of my clothes. My mother would not give them to him, saying that I should come home and forget what had happened. A brother-in-law sent me a few dollars, and he too urged me to return, reminding me of the biblical story of the 'prodigal son'. I thanked him, but said I would come back only after I had made a success of my life.

That is how things stood for this 17-year-old at the end of 1941. I could not afford newspapers, and had little interest in world affairs. I was too bound up with my own problems. But over the horizon events were taking shape that would affect the future direction of my life. War was about to engulf Malaya and Singapore.

INVASION BY THE JAPANESE

*As 1942 dawned, war came to Muar. I came face to face with
the grim realities of injury and death. And yet, I was able to take it all
in my stride. I felt I had little to lose. More importantly, perhaps,
I was too young to appreciate the dangers I was facing, and the
importance of the events I was witnessing.*

Towards the end of 1941, Muar was abuzz with rumours about the likelihood of war with the Japanese. The authorities were assembling a detachment of air-raid wardens. Because I heard they were offering two free uniforms, a pair of leather shoes and a small allowance, I volunteered. They rejected me because I was too small.

For a while life in the town went on mostly as usual. Then news spread that the Japanese had landed up-country, at Kota Bahru. We heard that they had bombed Singapore, but most people assumed that they would spare Muar, because there were no troops there other than a detachment of Johor military forces made up of Malays. There was even talk that they would also spare the whole of Johor, as the Sultan had earlier received a decoration from the Japanese emperor, and because there were several Japanese-owned iron mines and rubber estates in the state.

We were in for a shock. On 11 January 1942, Japanese aircraft attacked Muar with machine-gun fire and a few bombs. I was near the post-office when the attack came, and I jumped into a roadside drain for safety.

From that day onward, more and more people began to leave the town. Most of the rich Chinese had already left. Slowly, even the poorer families of all races began to move further and further inland to the kampongs off the main roads leading towards Batu Pahat and Bakri. Muar was turning into a ghost town, and there were outbreaks of looting, carried out by Chinese, Malays and Indians alike.

Nana and I decided to stay. Another friend of mine, Noordin, had moved to the interior with his family – they did not ask me to come with them as they themselves were not sure of finding a family to take them in.

It was clear that the Japanese army was about to attack. A detachment of Ghurkas passed through – the Ghurkas are famously tough Nepalese warriors, and traditionally many have served in the British army. When they saw us in the almost deserted kampong, they indicated that we should leave, firing a few rounds at the ground to get us moving, which we pretended to do, moving off the main road.

Muar town was bombed by the Japanese and people evacuated.

A few days after the bombing, larger number of other troops began to arrive, mostly Australians and Indians. Many of the Australians had got drunk on looted liquor. I remember them shooting wildly from their vehicles – they hit the house next door, and in one incident a child was injured.

At last, we decided we had to leave the town. Nana and I took the road towards Batu Pahat. At Parit Bakar, a few Indians in a Malay house asked if we wanted to join them. They did not know us, but seeing us trudging along with our possessions in small bundles over our shoulders, they obviously knew we were looking for shelter.

So for the time being we stayed with them. The oldest reminded us all that we were guardians of the place and should see to it that no damage was done to the furniture or other household possessions. We shared whatever vegetables there were and some salted fish, together with some rice, eating one meal each day.

On one occasion I went back into Muar with a member of the group called Peer, to look for some rice. On our way back, close to the Muar football ground, we heard the air-raid siren. Peer ran off towards a wooded area and I dived into a drain. At that moment a bomb went off nearby. When the all-clear siren sounded, I went in the direction Peer had taken, to look for him. There was nothing there but a large crater. He must have suffered a direct hit. There was nothing I could do but walk on back to my friends with the rice.

The Japanese finally captured Muar on 16 January. The Indian and Australian forces defending the town were virtually wiped out, and Australian reinforcements suffered terrible losses.

After rumours spread that Japanese soldiers had been seen in the town, we moved as a group to a house closer to the centre. Next day I dared to go out, and walked to the place where I thought Peer had been killed, hoping to find his body. Instead, I came across the body of a European soldier. The stench was

unbearable, and there were flies all over the corpse. For a moment, for the first time, I was gripped by fear, and the full realisation that I was in a battle zone.

One day I and some of my friends met a group of Japanese soldiers on bicycles. They were quite short – no taller than us, in fact. They looked pretty fierce, in their caps with cloth flaps hanging down behind, and rifles slung over their shoulders. They shouted at us: '*Kora kora!*' We had no idea what this meant. I assumed they were seeking directions, and so we pointed out the way into town.

I plucked up the courage to go into town myself. Many buildings had been burned out – in some areas the damage was extensive. There were dead bodies lying around on the ground, some of them civilians, some of them European soldiers. The smell was terrible. Most gruesome of all, at some junctions I saw severed human heads, stuck up on poles. Beneath them were cards, with Kanji characters written on them. They were warnings to would-be looters.

So the days passed. In the early days of the Occupation, there was not much to do, so my routine was to go to the barber shops at the ferry point, and while away the time with my friends there. Looking back now, my general attitude strikes me as amazingly laid back. I was prepared to take whatever fate had in store for me. Perhaps I was too young to recognise the full seriousness of the situation. Being Straits-born, I believed, like many other people (wrongly, as it turned out), that the British would soon take care of the situation and drive out the Japanese. I also consoled myself with the thought that, having so little, I had not much to lose, compared with many other people. I just lived from day to day.

A VISIT TO OCCUPIED SINGAPORE

*During February 1942, we heard that Singapore had fallen.
One of my friends in Muar, named Veeriah, decided that there might be
some commercial possibilities in the new situation. We had made a little
money selling cloth that we had taken from shops in Muar deserted
before the Japanese came, and we could use that for some trading.
To get to Singapore, we used pedal power.*

Three of us made the trip. We pedalled out of Muar, and by nightfall we had got as far as Kulai, where we slept the night in the five-foot way. Next morning we moved on towards Johor Bahru. We were regularly stopped and searched at Japanese sentry posts, and when we reached the Causeway we were told we could not cross without a permit.

We decided to try our luck again the next day. We spent the night at the Mariamman temple in Johor Bahru, where we begged some food from the priest, and slept on the floor. The electricity supply was down, and the entire town was in pitch darkness.

In the middle of the night we were woken by a loud shriek – a man near me was delirious and shivering. After some persuasion, including an oath of secrecy sworn before the temple deity, he told us what he had just seen. He had been working as a cook for a Eurasian family, who had taken refuge together with other Eurasians in the manager's bungalow on a rubber estate at Ulu Tiram, on the road to Kota Tinggi. A truckload of Japanese soldiers had arrived, and one of the men in the bungalow had shot at them. The Japanese soldiers returned fire, and then moved into the building firing indiscriminately in all directions. He ran and hid in the bushes behind the bungalow. Afterwards, when the soldiers had gone, he went back into the house. There he found a scene of carnage, bodies everywhere.

He ran out, walked some way and then hitched a lift on a lorry into Johor Bahru. As the sole surviving eyewitness to the massacre, he was terrified of what the Japanese might do to him if they found him.

The story was true. Months later I learned that several prominent Johor Eurasian families, including women and children, had been murdered on that estate.

Next day, we headed back through the town to the Causeway. My story this time was that we wanted to return to our families. I pleaded with a sentry using sign language, and words like 'mama' and 'papa'. He let us pass.

In those days part of the the Causeway was a section that could be raised and lowered to let boats through. The British had destroyed it after retreating into Singapore, but the Japanese had built a temporary bridge with planks. Embedded in the road were some metal, box-like objects intended to slow the Japanese motorised advance. Nobody stopped us at the Singapore end.

We cycled down Bukit Timah Road and Braddell Road. There were few signs of the earlier battle, which had been most intense on the other side of the Ford Factory. We headed for a kampong in Serangoon Road, near the junction with MacPherson Road. There, we dossed down in a cowshed next to the house of one of Veeriah's relatives. Over the next few days we managed to sell everything we had brought.

Then, without warning, there was a huge explosion in the distance, followed at intervals by several more – they went on for more than a day. We decided it was time to head back for Muar, taking some condensed milk and sardines we hoped to trade. Later we heard that the blasts came from a British ammunition dump at the Geylang English School in Geylang Road.

During our return trip, we passed a Japanese checkpoint on the coastal road in front of the Istana in Johor Bahru. The sentry insisted on confiscating my bicycle. I protested to one of his superiors, who pointed to a bicycle lying on the ground nearby in the checkpoint compound. It had a puncture. My friends persuaded me to take it, and we pushed it all the way back into town, looking for a bicycle repair shop. That took all day, so we spent the night in the town again. Next morning, mounted on a Royal Enfield bicycle (lady's model), I set off with my friends for Muar.

And what of my family in Singapore? Of course, I had been tormented by the desire to see them while I was there. However, I was afraid that if I went home, they would not let me leave, and I was still determined not to return until I had achieved something in life.

An encounter with Japanese soldiers at the Causeway.

ENCOUNTER WITH
THE JAPANESE ARMY

*While I was doing odd jobs as a hawker's assistant in Muar,
war came and my world changed. I had my first real contacts with
Japanese soldiers. While many Japanese behaved with great brutality
during the war, not all of them did, as my own experience showed.
Amidst the cruelty, I encountered one soldier who showed
compassion and concern.*

As I was whiling time away with friends, some Japanese soldiers asked for directions to the market. I showed them the way, and one officer, a second lieutenant, insisted that I stay and help them deal with the stallholders. He paid them in Japanese military currency. This became a regular event.

I came to know the officer as 'Amaya-san'. After a while he and some others gave me errands, such as buying pineapples, papayas or coconuts. They paid me in military currency plus packets of Japanese cigarettes. I was happy, as the cigarettes fetched good money on the black market.

Each day I would go to their camp and ask him and others if there were any chores to be done. One day, Amaya asked me why I wasn't learning the Japanese language. When I hesitated, he asked me my nationality. Up to now, being a Straits-born Indian, I had taken pride in my British nationality. Now I kept quiet about it, afraid that he might react badly, and that I might be put in prison. He asked about my parents. I said they were 'Indian'. He asked me why I was learning English. I said it was in order to earn a living. I might as well learn Japanese for the same reason, he said, as the Japanese were going to be around 'for some time'. Next time I saw him, he gave me an English-Japanese dictionary. With its help, and by picking up a few words from the soldiers, I gradually got the hang of the language. Although my Japanese was crude and colloquial, the errands became easier, and I earned more money, buying and selling fruit and cigarettes.

After a few weeks, Amaya-san introduced me to his superior, one Lieutenant Kokubu. He was older than the others, and conducted himself with a certain dignity. He never raised his voice, but he commanded respect and got things done.

Gradually I became indispensible to the company. Occasionally, when the soldiers had a day off, Kokubu would invite me to cycle with him into Muar. We would visit a Chinese eating shop, and he would order plates of noodles for both of us. He wrote his order on a piece of paper, as the Chinese could understand the characters.

One day I was asked to accompany Kokubu and a group of 50–60 soldiers on a work assignment. We set out on bicycles before sunrise. Near the village of Bakri, we stopped at a small government bungalow, where the men set about clearing undergrowth and shrubs. There was a terrible stench. Also working on the site was a contingent of Indian workers. They told me that the smell came from the corpses of soldiers killed in a clash between Japanese and Australian troops three

Japanese soldiers ask for directions to the market.

or four months earlier, the last major stand of the British troops at Bakri-Muar. The construction project was a Japanese war memorial. We made two or three such visits. I still have a photo of that memorial.

Lieutenant Kokubu gave me some advice that was valuable not only during the Japanese occupation, but also in later life. We were sitting in the shade of a tree, eating rice from a Japaneses *bento*, or food package. He asked me if I smoked, and he was pleased to hear that I didn't. He warned me of the dangers of *sake* (which in Japanese means alcohol in general). Then came a warning. Because of my ability to speak Japanese, and my contacts with him and his fellow soldiers, there would be people (he said) who would ask me to help them, and to do 'bad things'. He said I must always ask my conscience if anything I am asked to do is right or wrong. He was right to warn me. During the war many people tried to persuade me to do things that might have made me rich or have got someone else into trouble. Kokubu's advice gave me the determination to stand up to them and resist the temptation. It stood me in good stead after the war. There was no attempt by anyone to take revenge on me for working with the Japanese, including the Japanese civil police.

Later, he gave me advice about the use of authority. 'Be careful with power. It can sway one's head. Use power sparingly. If something can be done without using it, so much the better.'

I accompanied Kokubu and his military contingent when they were briefly posted to the state of Pahang. I acted as interpreter during a visit to the Sultan in the royal town of Pekan. Kokubu wanted to pay his respects, and ask for a loan of one of the Sultan's cars. I was very nervous about meeting royalty. He said the Sultan was just another man. The worst he could do was kill me, and unless I was going to harm him, that was not going to happen. I should not fear.

The visit went well. The Sultan himself treated me kindly. I was overwhelmed by the grand surroundings, and the range of dishes we were offered at lunch. Kokubu was offered a large American car, a Hupmobile, and enough petrol to get us to Kuantan. After a few weeks, when we were due to return to Muar, I arranged for the return of the car together with some extra drums of petrol. The Private Secretary expressed the Sultan's appreciation, saying that petrol was 'more valuable than gold'.

Two or three months later, although I had not asked him for help, Kokubu did me a final good turn, introducing me to the Japanese manager of a transport company, for whom I would be able to work as an interpreter and intermediary. After the interview, he told me that he would be leaving the following day. In the morning, I went to the camp to say goodbye. The site was deserted; the barbed wire fencing had all disappeared. The soldiers had gone during the night. Years later I was told by one of his soldiers that Kokubu had asked them not to let me know when they were leaving, as I would only feel sad.

It was many years before I met Kokubu again, but I always remembered his kindness and good advice.

The Sultan of Pahang graciously loaned us a car when I accompanied Lieutenant Kokubu on a visit.

EARNING A LIVING

It was through Lieutenant Kokubu that I found my first real job.
He made a special effort to ensure that I would be able to make
a living after he had gone — this persuaded me that there were
some well-intentioned individuals in the Japanese administration.
In the course of my work, first with a Japanese transport company
and later at the civilian police headquarters in Johor Bahru,
I discovered that for many local people corruption was
part of everyday life.

Before Lieutenant Kokubu and his regiment left, he arranged a job for me with a Japanese transport firm, the Tokyo Kyoko Company. He took me to see Mr Araai, the company manager, who told me to show my respect by bowing. He asked me in Japanese if I could read and write English and also if I spoke Malay. He said my job would be to help him interact with his two staff members, an elderly Chinese chief broker whom he called 'Ah Seng', and a clerk who only read and wrote Chinese.

I was to work for Araai as a personal assistant. He told me that I would be paid 100 dollars a month, a handsome sum at a time when prices were still about the same as at the beginning of the Japanese occupation, when Japanese currency was trading on par with British Malayan currency. I answered his telephone calls, especially if they were in a language other than Japanese. For a month or so there was not much to do. Then the work began to pick up. The company's job was to build up a fleet of haulage trucks. Initially it had only one three-tonner. Ah Seng, who was elderly but looked very tough, travelled around outside Muar, looking for lorries that were lying idle, hidden away in kampongs and on rubber estates. He would find the owners and persuade them to sell. He would first establish a price by bargaining in Hokkien and then return to Muar. He would then arrange for Araai to visit the location and seal the deal.

Because petrol was unobtainable, the owners were very happy to get rid of their vehicles, which were just rotting away. I was pretty sure that Ah Seng was making money from the sellers as well as acting for the buyer, by jacking up the prices, knowing that the company would probably pay whatever was asked. Araai obviously shared this suspicion, insisting that Ah Seng should not be within earshot when he was finalising the transaction. Corruption of this kind was very common during the Occupation. I had to be very careful not to get involved in it.

Gradually Araai's confidence in me as an honest employee grew. In early 1943, I helped him establish a new branch of the company at Batu Pahat, and two or three months after that, Araai's boss, by the name of Uchida, who was responsible for the whole of Johor, had me posted to the head office in Johor Bahru, where the company ran a fleet of taxis as well as lorries.

One day I had to go to the Vehicles Registration Office to sort out some problems concerning the registration of the company's vehicle fleet. It was in the same building as the police station. The source of the difficulties was the chief clerk, Mr Ratnam. He was tall and thin, a rather haughty individual. He was always puffing on a cigarette, issuing threats and shouting at everybody. Some other people visiting the counter told me that he tended to favour applicants with large vehicle fleets, who would bribe him with money and women. As evidence they pointed out the gold rings on his fingers, which were numerous and eye-catching. I was told that he was the only person who could approach the Japanese boss.

Ratnam was indeed a terror. When I was getting nowhere in my dealings with the counter staff I called out, asking if I could come into his room and speak to him. He shouted an answer sprinkled with four-letter swear words. I decided that I had had enough of that, and would try to see his Japanese superior. I found the officer's room in the police headquarters next door. His name was Ura. When I entered, he looked at me fiercely. Before he could raise his voice, I spoke in Japanese, apologising for troubling him. This took him aback, and with a smile he asked what I wanted. After asking where I had learned to speak the language, he called in Ratnam, and, in bad Malay, told him to deal with my requests. Any problems should be referred to him personally. Ratnam was furious.

I often had to visit the Vehicles Registration Office, and over time I got to know Ura quite well. He had been a policeman in peacetime, and had been seconded from Japan for service in Malaya. From time to time he would summon me to the police station from the transport company office, to help translate into Malay special instructions he wanted to give to the Malay police officers.

This started to cause friction between him and Uchida, the head of the transport company. I became the centre of a battle between them, when Ura asked for me to be released by the company so that I could work for him and the Inspector General of Police. I heard that harsh words were used. At last the dispute was resolved at a high level, and I was told that I was indeed to be transferred to police headquarters. At no time did anyone ask what I wanted – my personal preferences were not a factor in the situation.

And so I entered the employment of the Japanese civilian police, in which I stayed until the Japanese surrender at the end of the war. If I was able to earn respect, I did so by following the old saying: 'Honesty is the best policy.'

HOW THE JAPANESE RAN MALAYA

Working for the Johor police, I was able to see at first hand how the Japanese governed the state of Johor during the Occupation. They relied to a great extent on Malay officers for the running of the state, while Chinese police officers played an important role in anti-communist operations.

During the Japanese occupation, the state administration mostly followed the pattern already established by the British. The Sultan of Johor did not play a role, although the Japanese treated him with respect.

Although the *Gunseikanbu* (Japanese for 'Military Administration') in Kuala Kangsar reported to the Japanese army, it was run mostly by civilians. In fact, at least at the beginning, there was only a handful of senior Japanese in position in the state, and they were concentrated in Johor Bahru. However, there was a system of ranks for Japanese civilians which ran parallel to military ranks.

At the top of the Johor state administration was a Japanese governor, or *Chokang*, equivalent in rank to a military general. Reporting to him were the Japanese *Somuka*, 'administration department', responsible for the general running of the state; and also the office of the 'custodian of enemy properties'.

The civil administration, the departments that make up local government in peacetime, reported to the governor. The police did so in theory, but in fact they were semi-detached, reporting through a Japanese equivalent to the Inspector General of Police (IGP, or *keimubucho* in Japanese), to the state administration led by the governor, and also reporting separately to the military administration in Kuala Kangsar.

The Japanese spoke to one another in Japanese, which meant that no one else could follow their discussions in any depth. The working language at state and district levels was English, although some local officers spoke Malay among themselves. The Japanese used Chinese clerks to copy out documents by hand. A couple of Japanese-language teachers from Japan were posted to the teachers' training school.

Shortly after the arrival of the Japanese, a pro-Malay radical group, the Kesatuan Melayu Muda (KMM, or 'Young Malays Union'), ordered that all officials should speak and write Malay. To everyone's surprise the Japanese put a stop to that. All official communication, including basic documents such as utility bills, continued to be in English.

All local employees were paid in Japanese currency, although its value was eroded by inflation as the war went on. Some received extra rations in the form of cigarettes. Towards the end of the war a monthly ration of Japanese cigarettes sold on the black market fetched as much as a month's salary!

Few departments had Japanese officers posted to the districts. Hospitals and schools were all run by locals, as were services such as the water supply and electricity.

Whoever had some hands-on working experience in the power station, even if he had no formal qualifications, ran it. When water pipes were broken, local technicians were the ones to fix them. None of these services were overseen by Japanese officers – they were run by Malay members of the Johor Civil Service

The Kempeitai *frequently subjected local people to interrogation.*

and the Johor establishment, or by professionals and technicians of other races. The fact that locals were running the local administration was important practically and symbolically. We realised that we could do for ourselves many things for which, up to now, we had depended on the British. This increased our self-confidence when the question of independence came up after the war.

The first Japanese IGP was a military man, Colonel Tokizawa. His successors were all civilians seconded for service in Malaya from the domestic Japanese police. All the Japanese police officers were ranked one level above their rank at home.

Within the police department, there were two separate wings. One dealt with conventional police matters, and contained relatively few Chinese. The Chinese officers worked mostly in the other wing, dealing with 'peace preservation', focusing on anti-Japanese guerrilla activities, such as those carried out by the communist Malayan People's Anti-Japanese Army (MPAJA), which I shall describe later. Serious investigation of the communists was entirely in the hands of Chinese officers and detectives, who operated in outlying districts without much supervision.

Many Chinese officers worked closely with the state *Kempeitai* (Japanese military police), or, in districts where there was a Japanese garrison, with the army. They were in a strong position. The Japanese depended on them for intelligence. Some terrified the local population with arbitrary arrests and extortion. There were many opportunities for corruption. Many officers suspected of involvement in corruption became targets for revenge by the MPAJA after the Japanese surrendered at the end of the war.

My ability to speak some Japanese was a great asset to local police officers, especially those posted to the Districts. The police training school asked for my services more and more often as time went on. The recruits were mostly from rural areas, and I had to act as an interpreter, translating lectures from Japanese into Malay. Some of the Japanese lectures were about the way police officers should behave, using as a model the conduct of policemen in Japan, who, it was claimed, earned great respect. I was given a rank, *keibuho* (equivalent to inspector), as were most of the local officers. The authorities told me that this would help me interact effectively with uniformed personnel – it also meant an increase in pay and rations.

THE FORMATION OF THE MPAJA

When I was first engaged by the Johor Civilian Police Department, my role was to interpret instructions given by Japanese superiors to local officers and, later, police cadets. In 1943–5 I saw more of the effects of guerrilla action by the MPAJA. The origins of this organisation and the motives of its members give clues to the way Malaya's history developed during the postwar years. Communism remained a powerful threat in the form of terrorism and subversion well after independence into the 1970s.

The roots of the Malayan People's Anti-Japanese Army (MPAJA) lay in the Malayan Communist Party (MCP). The MCP was founded in 1930, under the direction of the Comintern, an international organisation dedicated to spreading communism across the world, which had set up the Communist Party of China in 1921. The MCP was an offshoot of the Nanyang Communist Movement. After the 1935 World Conference of the Comintern, the concept of the 'United Front' in Malaya (including Singapore) meant using trade unionism to paralyse industry and thus undermine the British and the economy on which the British depended; promoting a united front in racial and cultural terms as part of the struggle for self-determination; and mobilising opposition to the Japanese and later the elected governments of Malaya and Singapore. This was a feature of the communist threat to national security.

The MPAJA was set up immediately before the Japanese invasion of Malaya, with the reluctant agreement of the British. The British had been considering underground resistance to an invasion since 1940 and in early 1941 they set up a special training school for 'irregular warfare'; but their main military focus was on conventional methods. In July 1941, the MCP proposed to the British that they should work together in resisting the Japanese. It pressed the British to release all its members in detention at that time, so that they could be recruited into the resistance. In return the MCP would mobilise support for the British war effort.

The MPAJA trained in secluded areas of the jungle.

It was only in December, after a process of negotiation, that training of recruits started, and these became the core members of the MPAJA for the guerrilla struggle in Japanese-occupied Malaya of which Singapore was a part.

The MPAJA was in reality a Malayan Chinese-based organisation, although it presented itself as multiracial (its soldiers had three stars on their caps to represent the three races of Malaya – Chinese, Malays and Indians). People called it the 'Tiga Bintang' (Three Stars). In effect it remained predominantly Chinese with a sprinkling of Malays and Indians who sometimes joined it for anti-British nationalist reasons other than enthusiasm for communism, although in Malaya there was no deep-rooted Malayan national consciousness.

However, many Chinese still regarded China as their homeland, channelling their allegiance either through the MCP or through the Kuomintang (KMT, or Chinese Nationalist Party) which was active in Malaya. (Attitudes of Indians born in India or with links to India were similar.) Malay loyalty was centred on the ruler of each state. Loyalty to China was given an anti-British edge by a belief that China had

been humiliated by the West ever since the Opium Wars in the 19th century. The roots of the MCP's attitude towards the Japanese lay in the tensions between Japan and China that culminated in invasion by the Japanese in 1937. Some Chinese in Singapore and Malaya had actively supported China in that Sino-Japanese conflict. In the years just before the Japanese occupation of Malaya, there were organised moves to boycott Japanese goods, and attacks on Japanese shops in Singapore, including some in Middle Road. Active fund-raising for the war effort, in the form of the South China Relief Fund, was prominent in the major towns of Malaya and Singapore. There were efforts to raise volunteers to join the war as truck drivers, transporting supplies to China, and in other roles such as working on the Burma Road.

When the Japanese invaded Southeast Asia, their early moves to establish law and order after outbreaks of crime and looting involved summary executions and the display of severed heads on spikes. I had seen them myself in Muar and Johor Bahru. But the occupiers went further in their brutal campaign against the Chinese, and assumed that all Chinese were engaged in anti-Japanese activities. In fact, large numbers of Chinese played no part in such activities. But the Japanese treated them all alike: the Straits-born Chinese, the poor rickshaw-puller, the farmer, the shop assistant were all targeted for punishment. In the Sook Ching ('purification through cleansing') bloodbath of March 1942, thousands were slaughtered. The Sook Ching drove hundreds of young Chinese either into the ranks of the MPAJA itself, or into activities on MPAJA's behalf in towns and villages.

GUERRILLA ACTION

*The MPAJA used jungle-warfare tactics to resist the occupiers.
While I was accompanying the Inspector General of Police
(the head of the Japanese civilian police) in Johor
as an interpreter, a close encounter with the guerrillas
nearly cost me my life.*

It was not until late 1943, and especially 1944, that the Malayan People's Anti-Japanese Army (MPAJA) began to have any real impact. In the area around Muar, Segamat, Kluang and Batu Pahat, the MPAJA often attacked isolated police stations manned by Malay policemen and scattered communist leaflets before withdrawing to their bases in the jungle. Sometimes they would intimidate the population by killing one or two elderly Chinese men, and leaving their corpses in a public place where everyone could see them, with communist pamphlets strewn around their bodies.

The main coastal and other trunk roads along the west coast were relatively free of attacks, except for occasional forays intended as 'reminders' designed to frighten the population. The railway line was not sabotaged, nor were trains attacked as often as they were during the Malayan Emergency after the war.

In 1944, by which time I was working at the police headquarters in Johor Bahru, the MPAJA made a surprise attack on Segamat town in broad daylight, under the eyes of the Japanese garrison. This was daring, as there was a Japanese military garrison not far away. The day after, I accompanied the Inspector General of Police (IGP) to the scene. We were told that the guerrillas had briefly occupied the police station, and disarmed the officers there, without harming them. They had fired a few rounds into the air, and paraded up and down the street in whatever vehicles they could seize. By the time Japanese troops arrived, they had disappeared.

My services as an interpreter were in demand whenever the IGP travelled into the districts to be briefed by local officials on MPAJA activities.

Late that year I accompanied the IGP when he inspected a police post being created in the heart of the jungle area between Kota Tinggi and Kluang. We were accompanied by Malay and Sikh constables and a few Japanese police officers, as well as a contingent from the Singapore police. We travelled in motor launches up the river to Kankar Sisir. We moved on from the upstream landing point on

As I washed my face by the river, I discovered a wound on my neck.

foot. En route, I had my first experience of being bitten by leeches, which could get to your flesh even if your legs were covered by puttees (strips of blanket-type material, wrapped around the lower leg as part of the uniform). The treatment was to apply some cylinder oil, which made the leeches release their bite. After walking all day, we reached the operational headquarters of the MPAJA 4th Independent

Regiment. It was a generously laid-out camp consisting of attap-roofed buildings on a hillock overlooking a valley. The scene that awaited us suggested that the guerrillas had left in a hurry. There was a parade ground, a building that housed their training school, and various offices. Here and there were Chinese posters with sketches and inscriptions in Chinese, obviously designed to stir up strong anti-Japanese feelings in the men.

Two days later we headed back to the launch pick-up point at Kangkar Sisir. We must have got about half-way, around midday, when there was a burst of gunfire from a jungle-covered hillock. We all rushed to take cover. Our party returned fire and that was the end of the exchange. The IGP's samurai sword had been pierced right through by a bullet. When we reached the pick-up point, I splashed my face with river water. I felt a sharp sting on the right side of my neck. I thought it was the result of some kind of insect bite and paid no attention to it.

A few days later I went to the General Hospital at Johor Bahru to get some medicine for a cold. I mentioned the 'sting' to the doctor, a Dr Eapen, and he took a close look. He asked what I had been up to. When I told him, he said, 'My boy, you have been damned lucky! Had it been half an inch different, you would have been dead!' Using a hand mirror, he showed me three parallel, superficial wounds. Three bullets had grazed my neck. It was a very narrow escape. I was destined to live.

VIOLENCE AMONG
THE COMMUNITIES

The MPAJA were ruthless in their intimidation of local people.
Their treatment of the Malays in a particular Malay village in Johor
stirred up racial violence that disturbed people's lives and led to
revenge killings. As I travelled through the countryside with the
Inspector General of Police, I saw a shattered society.

One morning in May 1945, the Japanese Inspector General of Police (IGP) urgently asked me to travel with him in his car to Batu Pahat. He seemed worried. As usual, we had an armed escort. It struck me as strange that the first village along the Batu Pahat-Ayer Hitam road was deserted. Normally it was a bustling market place. The whole area from Parit Raja to a point just short of Batu Pahat town was eerily quiet, except for groups of men, women and children walking along the road in the direction of the town, carrying a few personal possessions.

When we reached Batu Pahat, the local police chief told us that race riots had taken place. Many people, both Malays and Chinese, had been killed. The trouble had started in Parit Raja. The Malayan People's Anti-Japanese Army (MPAJA) guerrillas had been harrassing the people of the village for money. It was a protection racket. They treated brutally anyone who resisted. We were told that the Malay women in the kampong were particularly fearful.

Some days before the riots, members of the MPAJA had insulted Malay villagers by occupying their prayer hall and slaughtering a pig. This was, we were told, the latest of a series of acts of this kind, although it was difficult to piece together the facts from the various versions of the story. When invading a village, the MPAJA were in the habit of heading for the nearest Chinese provision shop (every village had one), and from there fanning out through the village to look for the headman and other important Malay elders. This poisoned the relationship between the shopowners and the villagers. In the past, the shopkeepers had served as purchasers

of sheet rubber from the smallholders, and as providers of credit. Now, the villagers suspected them of co-operating with the guerrillas.

On the night when the prayer hall at Parit Raja was desecrated, the villagers had seen the guerrillas go to a Chinese shop. They then decided to take revenge on the shopkeeper. They murdered him and his family, children included. The effect was explosive, as village after village over a wide area became scenes of bloody acts of retaliation committed by both Malays and Chinese. Land was deserted and houses abandoned in a hurry. Poultry and goats were left to fend for themselves. People sought refuge in the two main towns, Batu Pahat and Pontian Kechil, while they waited for the return of law and order.

Looking back, I am sure that the communist guerrillas knew how people would react in anger to desecration of their religion. They saw the prospect of creating conditions that would bring about their notion of a revolutionary situation. It has been claimed that some actions, such as the pig slaughter, were carried out by Japanese pretending to be Chinese, so as to stir up feelings against the Chinese. I do not subscribe to that, as a Japanese, even in disguise, would not have been freely received by a Chinese villager. The guerrillas' visits to the Chinese shops and the reception they received persuaded the villagers of their identity.

After a briefing in the Batu Pahat police station, the IGP and the local police chief, also Japanese, conferred on the phone with the Japanese governor of Johor. Next day, I was told that a multiracial goodwill mission had been set up, with the mission of restoring peace among the communities.

The religious frenzy was reaching Batu Pahat, where even the young Malay policemen were already talking of a 'holy war' against the Chinese, casting all Chinese as 'MPAJA devils'. The MPAJA continued to exploit the unrest. A couple of weeks later, the goodwill mission while on tour was ambushed in Benut town. The MPAJA elements surrounded the local Chinese Chamber of Commerce, and attacked the group with automatic weapons. Some members were killed, others taken hostage. There was a real danger that racial clashes might escalate further.

One of those murdered was the district officer, a Malay. His replacement was Dato' Onn Ja'afar, who was later to have a distinguised political career as founder of

the United Malays National Organisation (UMNO). Dato' Onn joined discussions between Japanese and Malay officials about how to respond to the MPAJA activities. He took very seriously his responsibilty to restore law and order, and bring the administration of the district under control. In his first month as district officer, he went around on a motorcycle, talking to the people of each village, urging them to put away their distrust of one another, and live side by side as they had done previously. And within a month or so, a kind of peace was restored, although most Chinese decided to remain in the towns, despite the urgings of Dato' Onn, the *penghulu* (the traditional village heads) and leaders of the Chinese community in Batu Pahat. People of the area segregated themselves into Malay and Chinese communities.

An air of tension and uncertainty, and a few outbreaks of violence, persisted well after the British return to the same area at the end of the war. Law and order was fully restored only with the establishment of the postwar British civil administration in April 1946.

These events impacted me deeply. I was struck by the religious sensitivity of the Malays. If provoked, or not getting their way in matters of religion or race, they were inclined to take the law into their own hands, disregarding long-standing bonds with non-Malays or other groups in their neighbourhood. At the same time the MPAJA were ruthless and cynical in their provocation.

The lesson was clear. People who stir up trouble between the races know they are risking terrible consequences, and should be resisted by whatever means are available. In both Singapore and Malaysia, several outbreaks of violence were to take place in later years, showing very clearly what can happen when tensions get out of control. Race relations need to be carefully nurtured. Tensions have to be addressed as soon as they arise, before they result in violence and harm to peace and harmony.

HOW I BECAME
POLITICALLY AWARE

My family was local-born and not interested in politics. I considered
myself too unimportant for politics to matter. We took pride in our
pro-British affiliation. Two encounters with a charismatic leader of
the Indian independence movement changed my attitude.
That man was Subhas Chandra Bose.

In July, 1943, I first caught sight of Subhas Chandra Bose when he was arriving
for a meeting at the Istana Bukit Serene, a palace built by the Sultan of Johor
just before World War II, and occupied at the time by the Japanese military
commander for Southeast Asia.

Bose believed in armed struggle as a way of achieving independence for
India. He had been educated in higher studies in London, and could have joined
the élite Indian Civil Service, having excelled in the British qualifying exams.
Instead, he took up a political cause. He saw World War II, in which Germany and
Japan were both ranged against Britain, as an opportunity to bring independence
closer, and looked to Japan for support. He took over the leadership of the Indian
National Army (INA), which drew recruits mostly from Indian prisoners-of-war
in Southeast Asia held by the Japanese. His hope was that the INA could join with
Japanese troops in crossing the border from Burma into India itself, sparking a
mass uprising against colonialism by the Indian population, among whom he was
as popular as Gandhi.

I watched him get out of his car. He was bald, rather rotund, and wore glasses.
Japanese military officers stood at attention for him.

My Japanese boss, who was with me, told me that Bose was due, in a couple of
days, to speak on the Padang in front of what is now City Hall (the Japanese called
it Syonan Tokubetsu Shi). He suggested I go and watch the event. So, accompanied
by a politically active Indian friend, I did.

My friend and I arrived at the Padang at around 5.00 pm. Everywhere we could see flags of the Indian National Congress, a political party prominent in India's independence movement. The party still plays a leading role in Indian politics today. The whole of Singapore's Indian community seemed to be there. The front row of chairs were occupied by well-dressed couples from the élite.

Soon a line of limousines drew up, heavily escorted by cars carrying Japanese generals. The man I had seen at Istana Bukit Serene got out of one of them, and walked slowly on to the stage which had been set up on the steps of the City Hall. Everyone on the platform remained standing while he took his seat. Their behaviour suggested an attitude close to veneration. I waited with bated breath. I had never before seen Japanese people of authority show such formal and public respect, not even to the Sultan of Johor.

The time came for Bose to get up and speak. His first few words were in Hindi, a greeting to 'brothers and sisters'. After that he spoke in English. His theme was the

fight for India's independence. He spoke of British brutality, and massacres in which innocent people were machine-gunned. None of these incidents had been mentioned in my history lessons.

Soon it started to rain. Looking for shelter, the people in the seats began to move. Bose's voice boomed through the microphone. He said he had come a long way at great risk to himself, to pursue the struggle for independence. He was shocked to see people running at a sign of drizzle. He asked what the British had turned them into — so weak and cowardly! Were they not born with brothers and sisters? Did they not see it as their duty to liberate their struggling brothers and sisters from British bondage? The crowd quietly sat down again, and stayed in their places until the event was over and Bose left the stage.

This dressing-down impressed me. I was thrilled to see the élite getting such a tongue-lashing. Above all, I was impressed by the manner in which Bose had delivered the speech. Most Indians in Singapore spoke Tamil. Bose, who came from Bengal, did not (he did not speak Bengali very well either). He spoke off-the-cuff, and his English diction and delivery were perfect. This was the first time I had heard such references to history and the search for justice. He really fired my imagination, and

The crowd which came to listen to Bose speak was captivated by his rhetoric.

made me want to be active politically – and that led in the end to my support for the political struggle led by Lee Kuan Yew through his political rallies in the 1950s.

I met Bose briefly by chance a little later, when I was in Muar. I was accompanying a team providing an escort service for an unidentified, non-Japanese VIP, who turned out to be Bose, travelling up the peninsula. I went to catch a glimpse of the man himself. After he got out of his car, I walked beside him on to the ferry. 'You're Indian,' he said. 'Why don't you join the Indian National Army?' I replied, 'I'm local-born,' to which he retorted, 'What difference does that make?' I couldn't think what to say. At that point the ferry reached the other bank, and Bose continued on his way.

Bose did not have long to live. He is thought to have died in a plane crash on the way to Harbin in 1945. Nonetheless, he left behind an important political legacy. Years later, a BBC correspondent visiting the India-Burma border areas wrote that people in the Indian state of Manipur showed him the vast areas of the state that Bose's INA had occupied. They had hoisted the Indian national flag and declared it a liberated area, before being driven back into Burma.

Why was Bose important? He was fired by a passion I had never seen in others. His speeches were electrifying. He gave them in English. The vast majority of those who gathered to hear him were labourers and plantation workers, and their wives, comfortable only in their mother tongues. Yet even those who did not understand English stood for hours waiting to hear them. He showed how, with determination and passion, leaders can arouse a people. He seemed prepared even to give his life for his cause – that impressed us no end. His hopes for the Indian National Army were never fulfilled. However, his great Padang speech marked the dawn of mass politics among Indians in Malaya. Before him, only the Japanese – who had their own agenda – had spoken in public against British 'tyranny' and the need to fight it. No Chinese leader could have spoken out in this way, because of the strong anti-Japanese feelings among the Chinese. There was no Malay leader prominent enough to make such a speech. Whenever Bose spoke, there were reports in the papers. He created an atmosphere, which encouraged many people, including Malays and Chinese, to carry on their own struggles after the war ended, in activities such as the trade union movement.

I met Subhas Chandra Bose again in Muar when he travelled up the peninsula.

AFTER THE JAPANESE SURRENDERED

When the war ended, those who had worked for the Japanese feared for their lives. Emotions ran high, with good reason. Even today, it is hard to make sense of the way many Japanese behaved during the Occupation.

On 15 August 1945, the Emperor of Japan announced his acceptance of surrender terms. The news reached us in Johor five days later. The British arrived in Johor and Singapore on 5 September, and the formal surrender in Singapore took place a week later, on 12 September.

Before the British could re-establish their authority in Malaya and Singapore, there was a gap of around two weeks during which, throughout the state of Johor, the Malayan People's Anti-Japanese Army (MPAJA) effectively took control and terrorised the population in areas where there were no Japanese troops. Disregarding legal process, they held unofficial 'trials' as a form of revenge against those they suspected of 'collaborating' with the Japanese. All these activities led to further outbreaks of race riots, which they could not control. It was only with the arrival of the British Military Administration (BMA) in the rural areas that these efforts at retribution were brought to an end.

Throughout much of the Occupation, and particularly just after the end of the war, rumours circulated of appalling atrocities by the MPAJA. One of the guerrrillas' favourite forms of intimidation was to cut off one ear. I did not witness any such incidents personally, so my account is based on hearsay. Possibly some of the reports were exaggerated. But accounts of brutality, including such acts as digging out eyeballs and disembowelling, were so widespread at the time, that I took them seriously. I still do. My belief has been strengthened by eye-witness reports published since.

My last official duty for the Japanese Inspector General of Police (IGP) was to interpret for him when the son of the Sultan of Johor came to arrange for the Johor

After the Japanese surrendered, people hung the KMT flag, and celebrated in the streets.

state government to take over responsibilities from the Japanese. The IGP told him very politely that he had no orders as to such a handover, and until he had received instructions he would carry on as before. He gave an assurance that the Japanese would be responsible for law and order until the British arrived.

Once news of the surrender became public, all the shops in Johor Bahru were decorated with flags of the Kuomintang, as if to welcome Chinese troops. In the early days a few Chinese members of Force 136 (an underground force led by the British) were indeed seen in the town. The MPAJA were rushing around 'arresting' people and threatening reprisals, retreating hastily each time they encountered Japanese troops with fixed bayonets controlling the major road intersections. Malays were equipping themselves with parangs and in the kampongs there was a lot of

secretive discussion about resistance to the Chinese. When the British did arrive, the Indian and Malay populations in general felt a sense of relief.

I worried about my own fate. I had worked for the Japanese police, although I had never abused my position. As events turned out, I was never confronted by the MPAJA or anyone else. My relations with my Chinese neighbours in Johor Bahru continued to be friendly. My landlord at that time was an Indian shopkeeper with a Chinese wife. Next door on one side was a Chinese hotel, and on the other side was a Chinese hairdresser. They all knew I had worked for the police during the war, but I never sensed any ill feeling.

I have always accepted that my own experience during the Occupation was very different from the horrific treatment suffered by many at the hands of the Japanese army. I had seen the Japanese running Johor in a generally professional and fair way, relying mostly on the Malays and Indians to keep the administration going, and relying on the Chinese to deal with the communists. They had kept the administrative system set up by the British, including the use of English. Among them I met some highly cultured and civilised people. How was it that, at the same time, the Japanese treated so many people in Malaya and Singapore so brutally? How was it that so many Malayan labourers, and prisoners-of-war of many nationalities, died constructing a railway for the Japanese between Siam and Burma? I cannot reconcile that brutality with the qualities I found in some members of the Japanese civilian administration.

The principal villains among the occupying forces were the *Kempeitai*, the military police. In Singapore they numbered only a few hundred, but were supplemented by 1,000 or so auxiliaries, mostly young soldiers from the Hiroshima district, who were unsophisticated, uneducated, and willing to blindly obey orders, however brutal. While the Sook Ching operation in Singapore was not mirrored to any great extent in Johor, as far as I know, the number of deaths that resulted from that exercise was appalling. No one will ever be able to justify its brutality and arbitrary nature.

The contradictions will never be fully explained. However the story of the Occupation must remind us all never to be complacent, to be aware of the ability of human beings of all races and cultures to behave, in extreme circumstances, in ways that seem shocking, as we look back.

AN UNLIKELY FRIENDSHIP

My contacts with the British military authorities immediately after the war were not all happy, but they were not all bad either. I struck up a friendship with a young security officer who gave me some useful words of guidance – as well as a reference that later helped me get a job.

S oon after the establishment of the British Military Administration (BMA), I applied for a post as detective investigation officer in the Johor police. The Malay police who were fond of me urged me to apply. However, the interview did not go well. The interviewing officer – one Major Maclean – disapproved of my work as an interpreter for the Japanese during the Occupation, accusing me of being a collaborator. We also clashed over the Malayan People's Anti-Japanese Army (MPAJA) – he and many of his colleagues had an unrealistic, too rosy picture of their motives and record. I told him that one day, the British would discover the true nature of their new-found allies.

Corporal Evans asked if I could identify Japanese military police officers from pictures.

My next contact with the military authorities was very different. One day I was approached by a British Field Security Service officer. His name was Corporal Evans. He wanted to ask me some questions. We went to a nearby coffee-shop, and he asked me about my duties as an interpreter during the Occupation. I gave him a detailed run-down of my contacts with the Japanese, beginning with my life in Muar. He took detailed notes and left.

A couple of days later, he came back with some photographs of Japanese military policemen, and asked if I knew any of them. Not having worked with the *Kempeitai*, I could only identify one of them, a stout Japanese man with a walrus moustache. He was the *Kempeitai* head in Johor Bahru. I made the point that it was not only the Japanese who had behaved appallingly during the Occupation – much injustice and cruelty had resulted from the actions of Chinese officers in the force, as well as informers.

That was the beginning of a friendship that lasted until Evans left for Britain a month or two later. He cleared me from a security point of view, encouraged me to go on looking for a job, and offered to give me a reference. During those weeks we met often, spending long hours talking over coffee, noodles, curry and rice, or roti prata. I had no money, and he paid the bill.

Corporal Evans was very serious-minded. He talked at length about socialism. This was a time when socialism was a growing political force in Britain and many other countries – the general election in Britain in 1945 saw the socialist-inclined Labour Party defeat the Conservative Party led by war leader Winston Churchill. Evans was an admirer of Professor Harold Laski, a professor of political science at the London School of Economics. Laski was one of a group of left-wing academics who helped shape the beliefs of a whole generation of politicians, including some Singaporeans who studied in London and later became prominent in public life. They influenced English-educated political activists in Singapore, who had access to their publications in libraries.

Although I read the political pamphlets, I did not fully understand them. My educational record was feeble – I had only got as far as Standard Seven before the school threw me out, whereas Evans was ready to go to university after demobilisation. His knowledge of world affairs impressed me.

When the time came for him to go, he gave me a piece of paper, with some typewritten text on it. It was part of a speech by Abraham Lincoln. The words seemed to me to convey a profound message, similar to what my Japanese mentor Kokubu had taught me, but expressed more elegantly. From that day, throughout my working life, I carried these lines with me:

> *If I were to try to read, much less answer, all the attacks made on me,*
> *this shop might as well be closed for any other business.*
> *I do the very best I know how — the very best I can; and I mean to keep*
> *doing so until the end.*
> *If the end brings me out all right, what is said against me won't*
> *amount to anything.*
> *If the end brings me out wrong, ten angels swearing I was right would*
> *make no difference.*

Before he left, Corporal Evans gave me words of encouragement.

WHO DID WE THINK WE WERE?

As a young man I always saw myself as a Malayan. My Indian background was secondary. The political changes that followed the end of the war challenged my sense of identity. Plans for the Malayan Union and the Federation of Malaya separated Singapore from the rest of Malaya, a split that became final in 1965. I still regret the divorce.

The end of the war brought a new political era. Politics was in the air. The British Military Administration that followed the Japanese surrender came to an end on 31 May 1946. The British replaced it initially with the Malayan Union, which included the former Federated Malay States, Non-Federated States, and Straits Settlements – excluding Singapore, which, having been one of the 'Straits Settlements', now became a separate crown colony. Britain considered Singapore to be strategically important for the protection of British interests in the region, including Malaya and the Borneo territories; and also feared that the large Chinese majority in Singapore might unbalance the whole Malayan Union scheme.

The thinking behind the Malayan Union was to give equal treatment in Malaya to all three major races – Malays, Chinese and Indians. It would have removed the sovereign status of the individual states, and restricted the role of the Malay sultans, who were to be left in charge only of Islamic matters and Malay customs. The Malays greeted it with fierce hostility. They feared the loss of Malay power in their homeland. Malay nationalism was becoming a force to be reckoned with. Public rallies were held in various parts of Johor and in the non-federated Malay States, including Kedah, Perlis, Kelantan and Trengganu. Political parties called protest meetings. The United Malays National Organisation (UMNO) came into being as a voice for Malay opposition. It was joined by other Malay organisations.

At that time I had not formed any clear political views. If I felt anything, it was that the Malayan Union would be good for non-Malays. I think many non-Malay people in Johor would have liked to see it continue.

The Malays protested in the streets against the Malayan Union.

As 'Malayans', we non-Malays distinguished ourselves from India Indians, or China Chinese. When the Malayan Union excluded Singapore, we were mildly disappointed. I regarded myself as a 'Singapore-born Malayan', and I would have liked to have seen Singapore inside it, as would many other people in Singapore. When the British embraced UMNO as their main negotiating partner, we were really concerned. A distinguished Malay friend of mine told me not to worry – he said we should interpret UMNO as 'United MalayAN National Organisation'. In fact the 'M' stood for 'Malays', and still does.

In the face of vehement opposition to the Malayan Union, the British backed down. Fresh agreements were negotiated in discussions in which UMNO played a prominent role. The status of the state rulers was to be restored, as were the special position and rights of the Malays. On 1 February 1948, the Federation of Malaya came into being.

At that time, I was still in a mainly Malay environment, and did not really think through the relationship between the Malays and other groups. We operated like equals, and I expected that situation to continue. My main complaint was the introduction of identity cards, which, because we had to specify our 'race', looked like an unwelcome attempt by the British to intrude into our privacy. Now I can see their value. The guerrillas could not obtain identity cards, a fact which helped the authorities identify insurgents during the Emergency. They really were cards in those days, not plastic, but they did carry one's photograph with an embossed stamp.

The Federation of Malaya agreement was signed by the sultans in 1948.

At the same time the communists, who had formerly been allies of Britain in opposition to the Japanese, now became their fierce opponents. The months immediately after the establishment of civil administration were marked by constant communist-led protest meetings and rallies called by organisations allied to the communists. These seemed to be happening at the drop of a hat. Communist activists were all over the place, their leaders throwing their weight around. Every opportunity was taken for a display of defiance against British authority.

In private, the communists and their supporters would claim that they were working for the common good of all races, as represented by their three-star emblem. I was sceptical. It was clear that they were trying to get support among non-Chinese for the communist cause. They must have assumed that people like me and some of my friends, having lost our jobs at the end of the war, were likely to be anti-British. They were not totally mistaken – many former Indian National Army members took part in agitation on the rubber estates before the Emergency was declared in 1948, and an open fight against the communists took place in earnest.

Meanwhile daily life went on, and by this time I was working for the Johor Public Works Department.

KNOCKING ON THE
THE CIVIL-SERVICE DOOR

*After the war ended, I needed a job. And when times are tough, as
they were during the postwar military administration, you cannot be
too fussy. You have to take whatever is available. Later, in order to get
into the Johor Civil Service, I had to take a cut in salary. It was a gamble,
but it was the right decision.*

Through a friend who worked in the Johor Bahru labour exchange, I heard
of a vacancy at the workshop that maintained motor vehicles for the British
Military Administration (BMA). I applied for the job, got it, and began
work as a financial clerk at a salary of $80 a month, on a month-to-month basis.

In charge of the garage was a kindly old soul, a British officer by the name of
Captain Carpenter, who obviously knew nothing about cars. He would make a show
of going underneath vehicles when all he had to do was lift the bonnet — but he left us
to get on with our work, and the team was a happy one. Among my fellow workers
was Bob Cornelius, who later became a motorcycle ace; and Wong Nguk Lai, whose
brother, Wong Ngit Liong, later became chairman of the NUS Board of Trustees.

After a few months, when the BMA was about to end, I was offered a job in
the Johor Public Works Department, at an even lower salary, again on a temporary
basis. Against the advice of my friends, I decided to take it. And so, in 1946, my
civil-service career began — albeit still in Johor rather than Singapore. The fact
that I did not have the required qualifications — those that certainly would have
been necessary before the war — did not seem to matter. The British return had
the unexpected effect of opening up jobs to people like me. Many people had had
their education disrupted, and so relatively few had the right qualifications. In this
way unpromising circumstances can throw up unexpected opportunities.

The next year, my position became permanent. I was lucky. According to the
regulations, the Johor Civil Service employed only subjects of the Sultan of Johor.

Working for the Johor Civil Service.

Even Malays born in Malacca were ineligible. But times were changing, and I had the support of the chief clerk, T. Chelvathurai, and a senior Malay officer, Tuan Haji Annuar Malek – both of whom I had got to know earlier, during the Occupation. I learned very early on the importance of mobilising support when progressing one's career.

In those days, the office environment was very different from today. I remember a team of typists with big, heavy, manual typewriters, and a huge volume of paper. There was no air-conditioning – to keep cool we relied on ceiling fans and natural ventilation.

Although officially I was working in the financial section, from time to time I had to help out with personnel work. This is how I got involved in negotiations over pay for civil servants, as I picked up expertise on salary scales, and rules and regulations affecting government employees. It came as no surprise when the leadership of the Johor Civil Service Association (JCSA) asked me to help them. This staff organisation was not yet a registered trade union.

The leaders were determined to fight the 'back pay' issue – the fact that in calculating wages to compensate for the period of the Japanese occupation, British

officers were given a much better deal than the one offered to local employees. Arguments on this and related issues dragged on for years, causing great resentment, and led many white-collar government workers into political agitation against the British. I helped in articulating our grievance and continued to take part in the debate with British officialdom.

I helped the association leaders prepare their case when a government Salaries Commission began to look into civil service conditions in 1946, and failed – as we saw it – to establish equality of treatment as between locals and expatriates. Another commission in the 1950s similarly failed to meet our objections. Although it abolished the British officers' Children's Allowance entitlement, to which there was strong local objection, it consolidated Expatriate Pay for British officers as part of their salaries.

In 1950, the JCSA became a registered trade union, and I became its secretary. The union president, Ungku Aziz, and I decided to link up with public service trade unions in other parts of the Federation of Malaya. That way, we got to know a number of people who later played an important part in Malayan politics. At that time, when the Emergency was at its height, there was not yet much trade unionism in the limited amount of industry that then existed. Industrialisation had not really begun in Malaya. The postal, railway, and rubber plantation workers were the most prominent organised groups. They were led mostly by Indians, some local-born Chinese, and Malays at the working level.

I knew that, unlike my colleagues, I did not have a Cambridge School Certificate (the equivalent of 'O' levels today). This motivated me to try harder, and work longer hours than the others. The knowledge of English I had gained at school was useful – the British engineers who signed outgoing letters and communications with higher authorities noticed my work, and they turned to me when they wanted something expressed particularly well.

I learned a lot from my boss, a Eurasian named J.A. Buxton. A master of diplomacy, he showed me how to handle delicate matters such as proper accounting for funds paid by the federal government to the state to support the drive against the communists. These expenses were not audited, and presented opportunities

Ibrahim Hamzah designed the Malaya flag.

for fraud. I remember rolls of barbed wire travelling around the state being 'installed' several times over, with a lucrative invoice being raised each time. Many military and civilian officers holding high positions made money this way. I had to help counter several such scams, with limited success. Corruption was widespread during the BMA period, as it had been during the Occupation.

In my dealings with personnel issues, Buxton taught me an important lesson. One should never despatch memos written in the heat of the moment. One should not allow emotion to creep in. A harsh tone only leads the other side to dig in his or her toes.

On the other hand, principles matter. I remember an argument between a senior British executive engineer and the state's resident commissioner, the highest British officer in the state. It related to back pay claims by two Indian employees, penalised for their former involvement with the Indian National Army. The engineer marched to the commissioner's room, taking me along with him, and protested strongly, using colourful language. I feared he might be punished for insubordination. A couple of days later, we learned that the claims had been reconsidered, and accepted.

This episode taught me that not all colonial officers were unjust, and that some would stand up on grounds of principle, especially the Scots. Although warning me not to get carried away, the engineer told me that one should not be afraid to speak one's mind when something was wrong.

I witnessed an interesting piece of history, the designing of the Federation of Malaya flag. Dato' Onn and Haji Annuar gave the task to one of my colleagues, a draftsman called Ibrahim Hamzah. The instruction was to follow the general design of the US flag. The 'star' motif came from the flag of the Johor sultan.

THE MARIA HERTOGH RIOTS

One of the most serious outbreaks of public disorder in postwar Singapore showed how insensitive or inflammatory press reporting at times of heightened religious tensions can have disastrous consequences.

In 1950, when I was working for the Public Works Department (PWD) in Johor, I took night classes in Middle Road, Singapore. I went down on the bus which terminated at Queen Street. One day I arrived as usual at around 6.00 pm, whereupon we were all told to go home immediately, because rioting had broken out in the neighbourhood. Later I found out from the radio, and from my brother who had encountered a violent mob on his way home from work, what had happened.

The trouble started outside the Supreme Court building, and had spread across town to the Sultan Mosque area and to Geylang, further east. It was sparked off by a judicial decision concerning a young girl, Maria Hertogh. She had been born some 13 years earlier to a Catholic couple living near Bandung in Java. Her Dutch father, serving in the Dutch army, was interned by the Japanese in 1942. Although details of what happened then were disputed, Maria lost contact with her mother and ended up in the care of one Aminah Mohamed. Cik Aminah brought Maria up as a Muslim.

After the end of the war, Maria's natural parents asked various authorities to help find her. She was located in 1949, and a battle for her custody took place in the Singapore courts. Aminah was backed by M.A. Majid, president of the Muslim Welfare Association, with whom I was to have a difficult relationship later when working as a seamen's welfare officer. While the legal exchanges were going on, Maria was married, according to Muslim rites, to a trainee teacher by the name of Mansoor Adabi. The court in Singapore declared her Muslim marriage invalid, as she had not reached the age of consent under Dutch law, and determined that she should be returned to her Dutch father. Fortunately for him, Mansoor had been advised not to consummate the marriage. Years later he said to me, 'I'm damned lucky I didn't do it.'

Maria was moved for her safety temporarily to a Catholic convent. Journalists and photographers got into the convent, and on 5 December the *Singapore Standard* published a photograph of Maria holding hands with the Reverend Mother. Reports began to circulate that she had knelt before a statue of the Virgin Mary, although no such picture has ever come to my notice.

Muslims were outraged. When the court's decision to return Maria to her mother was finally confirmed on appeal, a crowd of over 2,000 gathered outside. For three days, rioters attacked Europeans and Eurasians on sight. Eighteen people were killed and 173 injured.

Maria Hertogh with Aminah Mohamed.

I believe the authorities had underestimated the power of religion – this became, at heart, a religious issue, not a communal dispute. Later, when I was studying at university, I became more aware of the role the press had played. The leader of the protesters was one Karim Ghani, an Indian Muslim with a history of activism in Burma and Malaya. He had been the 'Information Minister' of the 'Indian Independence Government' of Subhas Chandra Bose. He was the editor of a Tamil newspaper, *Malaya Namban*, which ran critical coverage, as well as an English-language paper, *Dawn*. The main Malay paper at the time, *Utusan Melayu*, printed in Jawi, had printed inflammatory reports. The Roman-script *Berita Harian* had not yet appeared. It was not easy for the authorities to monitor the press for incitements to disorder, or even the misrepresentation that was common also in the Chinese-language press. The *Indian Daily Mail* had also played a part in stirring things up. One of the English-language *Singapore Standard* reporters on the story was an expatriate who, as I found later when I was secretary of the University Socialist Club, had a habit of misrepresentation.

The Maria Hertogh riots demonstrated how irresponsible reporting by the press at sensitive times can have tragic consequence. Religious and racial harmony may prove all too fragile. It is easy to arouse passions by agitation over religious issues. In multiracial and multi-religious Singapore, it could lead to violence and conflict, as has happened in the past. Showing respect, understanding and tolerance for other faiths is essential to the preservation of our racial and religious harmony and our survival as a nation.

The Maria Hertogh case demonstrated how religion can become a divisive issue.

SELF-IMPROVEMENT AND THE PATH TO UNIVERSITY

Throughout my life I have been very fortunate in the mentors who have crossed my path. Once I realised that indeed I had abilities, as the Japanese had told me, I was driven to aspire to higher things. Early on, I also discovered the value of hard work, through which one can achieve much, however great the obstacles may seem. It was largely through sheer effort that I finally found my way to university as a mature student, nearly 10 years after the war.

Although I did not have any formal educational qualifications, and felt a little insecure, I believed in my own potential. So, I worked hard in my job at the Johor Public Works Department, and made a good impression on my superiors, including the British engineers who headed the department and its various sections. I tried to be more useful than my colleagues, and often worked longer hours than they did. I gained experience in various types of work relating to accounts and personnel.

I had never sat for the Cambridge School Certificate, the equivalent of today's 'O' levels. Taking the exams at this stage of my life seemed, at first, quite out of the question, because of the long hours I had to spend in the office and in union work. But I also knew, as I had during the Occupation, that I had the potential to learn. My self-belief was reinforced by the outcome of the state-wide government exams that enabled clerical officers to move up the salary scale. The exams for Johor were held anually. When the results came out, I learned that I had come second in the whole state, just one mark below the top candidate, a Malay.

Although I knew that as a non-Malay, I would never be able to get beyond the 'clerical service' grade into the 'Johor Civil Service' proper, I decided to improve myself anyway. I took evening classes in typewriting and book-keeping, and passed the London Chamber of Commerce exams with distinctions. My book-keeping

teacher, one Soo Ho Kum Chin, encouraged me to take classes in higher typewriting and accounting, and for these I had to go down to Singapore, at the Singapore Institute of Commerce, in Middle Road. It was there that I first met P.S. Raman, who in later life went on to be Singapore's ambassador to Indonesia and the Soviet Union.

I caught up on my studies early in the morning before leaving for work.

Finally, I decided to take the plunge, and study for the Cambridge School Certificate through a correspondence course offered to students all over the world by Wolsey Hall, Oxford. Perhaps the fact that my fiancée had completed the exam made me realise that absence of qualifications might affect my chances of winning her hand. My dedication was tested to the utmost. For a whole year I got up every day at 4.00 am, and studied for three hours or so before going to the office. By that time I was already getting involved in trade union matters, which took up the time between leaving work and having dinner. I was in bed by 8.30 pm most days – there was no time for entertainment, no free evenings. I would send my work off to Oxford by surface mail, and two or three weeks later it would come back duly marked. At last, in December 1951, I sat for the exam and was awarded a Grade II certificate, better than I expected.

This really boosted my confidence. Before that, going to university had been no more than a dream. Then, my friend Ungku Aziz, who was by this time lecturing at the University of Malaya in Singapore, told me about a new diploma course in Social Studies there. Mature students could be admitted, subject to an admission exam.

Ungku Aziz was persistent in encouraging me to apply. What about money? I had only the salary brought in by my job, and no savings. He reasoned that I might be able to get a scholarship, if I was offered a place on the course. He would not take 'no' for an answer – I should put in an application and worry about the money later. And so I applied.

I was accepted. With no solution to the money problem in sight, I started the process of applying for no-pay study leave from the Johor government, and permission to take my entitlement of half-pay for six months. My faith was rewarded. By the time I left Johor Bahru for the university, where I had accepted the offer of a room at the newly built Dunearn Road Hostels, I had been awarded a Shell bursary for $2,000 a year for two years.

I looked forward to my university studies with a mixture of pride and apprehension. While others had given me moral support, I had gained this opportunity through sheer hard work, having started out with no qualifications at all. The lesson I draw is that it is always possible to move forward, provided one makes the effort. I also learned the value of encouragement, which is why, since then, I have always tried to encourage others as they try to build their own careers, no matter where they have started from.

UNIVERSITY LIFE

*During my childhood, my education was cut short. At university
I was able to catch up. There, I learned about social work. More
importantly, the course taught me how to study and think for myself.
It taught me to go on learning.*

I started my course at the University of Malaya in 1952, at the age of 28. All but one on the course had work experience, and were older than most of the other students. Most of them had been sent on the course by their employers and were on full pay. The teaching staff came from the departments specialising in the individual subjects that made up our course, except for a few specialising in Social Work and Psychology.

Our daily routine involved lectures and tutorials – something we had not experienced before – and study in the library. Once the lectures were over for the day, we would gather in the canteen, as most of my group were living off-campus. Some of them were married, with family obligations. I lived at the Dunearn Road Hostels, known today as College Green.

University teaching methods seemed strange at first. During my school days I would absorb the content of a lesson, and simply regurgitate the facts later, when asked. Now I needed to form a deeper understanding of the subject, and get to grips with different ways of looking at it.

Economic social history, in the form taught to us, was mostly UK-centred. At first we could not see its relevance to our local situation. Later I changed my opinion. It was indeed relevant. Problems of poverty, injustice and cruelty occur in all societies. In Britain they had led to social reforms which tackled some of the effects of large-scale exploitation of young and old, unemployment and other ills, and laid the foundations of the modern welfare state. In later years Singapore adopted its own approach to these issues, but it was important for us to understand them. Learning about the effects of the Industrial Revolution (which took place in Britain

in the late 18th and early 19th centuries), and the accompanying exploitation of workers, gave me a better understanding of the rationale behind trade unionism, which the British Labour government encouraged in postwar Malaya.

We all attended tutorials together. We had to read widely, and were given lectures by distinguished experts. One of them was Dr Goh Keng Swee, whose subject was statistics. This is a complex subject. Dr Goh's efforts to simplify it for our benefit were not entirely successful – moreover, as other students have recorded, his low voice and monotonous delivery combined with the heat of the afternoon after lunch led to a certain drowsiness in his listeners. Dr Ahmad Ibrahim, the state advocate-general, was a brilliant lawyer, but his delivery was marred by a stammer, and often we could not resist the temptation to supply the word he was obviously trying to get out. But these were minor obstacles, and gave us cause for amusement.

The lectures described social deprivation that was many times graver than anything I had experienced myself. After a year or two, we understood that we were being trained to look at problems and their causes dispassionately, and think out ways of solving them, without being driven by our own emotions. I learned how to analyse human behaviour, which helped me see through the political agendas of many fellow students and people I encountered later in the world of industrial relations. For these insights I will always be grateful to the university. Without this general grounding I am sure I would never have progressed as far in life.

Each of us was given individual attachment programmes for practical experience. One of mine was to investigate labour problems in the city council's health, city cleansing and labour welfare departments. Longer attachments took place during the annual long vacation. At the end of my first year I was sent to Malacca, to work with the British Red Cross. They had a unit doing medical relief work in various parts of the state, which was still under Emergency rule. Some of the cases I saw were heart-rending – it was very difficult to be emotionally detached. I remember going to a rubber estate, and meeting two children, one about seven years old, the other about twelve. Their mother had passed away long before, and their father had just died of tuberculosis. How were they going to find anything to eat? I did what I could, which was not much, in the limited time I had.

Looking back I can see that going to university was a true intellectual beginning. It made up for everything I had missed during my school days. People often say that its greatest value is not the factual information you store in your head. This was certainly true in my case. It taught me how much I did not know, and how to study. Learning became a habit, a continuing quest for understanding. Knowledge gained from wide reading helped me in my various later careers, when I had to chart my own course without a properly defined brief.

University life forges bonds that last a lifetime. Today the mere mention of Dunearn Road sparks off memories in the the minds of everyone who ever lived in the hostels, whether during my time or later. I knew that some of my friends would go on to be senior teachers or school principals; some would follow an academic career in the universities; some would be doctors; many of the outstanding scholars would rise up through the civil service. Whatever paths they chose, I was sure that the bonds I had forged with them would endure.

Time proved me right. For example, when I was posted to Malaysia as Singapore's High Commissioner, these links opened doors, and enabled me and Malaysian officials to resolve many problems on a friendly basis.

THE PITFALLS OF STUDENT POLITICS

My diploma course at the University of Malaya brought me into contact with left-wing politics. I learned that one has to be cautious in choosing one's political associates. My final exams coincided with some dramatic events, and a police interrogation.

The Dunearn Road Hostels were abuzz with political chatter, as the Emergency in Malaya was beginning to wind down, and people were thinking ahead to the time when Malaya would achieve self-government and, in due course, independence from Britain. Students educated in Chinese schools and/or gripped by the anti-Western political rhetoric in mainland China were the most anti-British. Others opposed colonial power in principle.

Some of the strongest views were held by the medical students. Several were among the group that, in February 1953, formed the University Socialist Club. The first club meeting included some individuals who played important roles in Singapore politics in years to come. They included James Puthucheary and Sidney Woodhull, who both went on to be radical trade unionists and political activists. Woodhull was the first publications secretary. Wang Gungwu, later a distinguished academic, was elected the first president.

The Chinese school agitations of 1953 raised the political temperature. Different groups debated whether and how they should show solidarity with the students at Chinese High and Chung Cheng middle schools who had locked themselves inside their compounds.

During my second year I became secretary of the University Socialist Club, with the routine tasks of calling meetings and taking minutes. Puthucheary and Woodhull were still members of the central working committee; others included Hashim Sani, who later became chief justice in the Malaysian High Court. The year

before, the club had tried to raise its profile by publishing a magazine, *Fajar* ('dawn' in Arabic), although it didn't gain a very wide readership. Part of my job now was to bring in advertisements to cover *Fajar*'s printing costs.

As the year wore on I was concerned about the club's political direction. We began to hear gossip about 'tea parties' at Paterson Hall, the hostel for medical students. I had the impression, based on what Puthucheary said about these gatherings, that they might be communist 'cell' meetings. An air of secrecy surrounded them. There was talk of a young lawyer, Lee Kuan Yew, and his sympathies for the Chinese school students and for radical politics in general.

A group of us began to ask ourselves if we were getting tangled up in something we had not intended, working for a communist cause in the name of socialism. I wondered if Lee Kuan Yew could be a 'fellow traveller', a secret communist sympathiser. It was only later, when the People's Action Party was engaged in an open struggle to win support from the masses that we understood Lee's long-term political strategy, and the need, as he described it, to 'ride the tiger' of the left.

So I stepped down as secretary, although I remained on the club's central committee, continuing to pull in advertising for *Fajar*.

Soon, it was time for my final exams. Because of the work pressures many of us faced, the task of publishing *Fajar* was given to an editorial board made up mostly of people who had no exams that year. Unfortunately they allowed an issue to appear containing a provocative editorial with the headline 'Aggression in Asia'. This provoked a tough response from the authorities, in the form of a sedition charge against the editorial board, including Woodhull.

One morning, a couple of days before my exams ended, I woke up to find that during the night our hostel had been raided by the police. My table was a mess, my papers were strewn all

over the place, and drawers had been opened and emptied. My room-mate, Lee Ah Chai, said that the police had told him not to wake me up. Several students had been hauled off to the headquarters of the police Special Branch for questioning.

A day or two later, I was summoned to the Special Branch office in Robinson Road (where Capital Tower is now). After a long wait, I was questioned by an angry-looking Indian police officer, Ahmad Khan. He demanded to know anything I could tell him about the University Socialist Club. After an interrogation, I had to make a statement. In it I said that I was opposed to communism and not inclined to support communist or left-wing causes. I was allowed to go, but was told that I might be wanted for further questioning or to appear in court.

So the term ended, and I left the hostel to start my practical social work assignment for the year. This took me to Alor Star, Kedah, for six weeks.

I had attended university on the basis of no-pay leave. After returning from Kedah after finishing my course, I was posted by the Johor public

I joined the University Socialist Club.

I was interviewed at the Special Branch Office of Police.

service temporarily to Kluang, where I waited nervously for my exam results. The news was good – I had achieved my diploma in social studies. Shortly afterwards, my diploma was upgraded to a Diploma with Distinction.

In August 1954, the *Fajar* trial took place. Many people, even in government circles, were not convinced that the prosecution was wise or justified. Lee Kuan Yew acted as legal advisor to the University Socialist Club, and he arranged for a Queen's Counsel (a senior-ranking lawyer in the British legal system in force at the time) to defend the students, while he himself acted as junior counsel.

The students were acquitted. However, my experience in student politics led me to be mindful ever since that while in politics you may be sleeping on the same bed, others may have different dreams, not what you think they are.

HOW I MET MY WIFE
— AND FINALLY MARRIED HER

My wife and I have enjoyed a long and happy marriage.
The story of our courtship and engagement is one of persistence
against the odds. It began during the Japanese occupation.

You could say that I married the girl next door, but it took me 16 years to do it. During my childhood in Muar, the adjoining shophouse was occupied by a family headed by one K.P. Nandey, a man with a fiery disposition who tended to smash plates when in a temper. Later, during the Occupation, when I was back in Muar alone, I became friendly with one of the sons of the family. One day, when visiting him, I caught sight of his sister standing at the window of their house. Her name was Urmila, or 'Umi' for short.

Before long, while running errands on my bicycle for the Japanese soldiers, I started regularly to go out of my way, so that I could pass the front of the house. I only possessed one good shirt at that time. It was mauve in colour, and it made quite an impression on Umi, or so she tells me.

Umi's parents would not have seen me as a suitable match. My family origins are Tamil. They were Bengali, and they would no doubt have preferred a Bengali suitor, ideally a nice lawyer or doctor. So I started to leave her notes. She would leave her reply, and I would sneak by and collect it.

In due course the family decided to move to Johor Bahru, by which time I was already living there myself. To ingratiate myself I borrowed a truck from my Japanese employer and moved their household possessions overnight. From then onwards, Umi's father looked on me a little more kindly.

My relationship with Umi's brother soured – he did not approve of my interest in his sister.

In 1952, Umi applied for a teacher-training course in Britain that would take her away for two years. She was awarded a place, and was all set to leave in August,

two months before my own university course started. I think her father was happy to get her away from me for a time.

Her leaving was very painful. She was set to fly from Singapore to Kuala Lumpur, where she would meet up with her Malayan fellow-students before flying on to London. Since we could not meet openly in Singapore, after she took the flight to Kuala Lumpur, I travelled up there myself, where we met and then parted tearfully. We had a photograph taken, showing us together, and vowed to keep in touch by letter.

I was deeply saddened, and cried all the way on the flight back to Singapore. My mother consoled me later, saying: 'Don't be sad. Leave it to God. If he wills, all will turn out according to both your wishes.' And it did.

Umi and I secretly kept in touch in the early days of our relationship.

I saw Umi off at the Kuala Lumpur airport, from which she took a flight to the UK for her teacher-training.

While she was away in the UK, we kept up with weekly airmail letters. I was always anxious, as I was afraid she might come into contact with someone better than me. It did not happen. She was as steadfast as on the day when we parted.

When Umi returned, her father invited me to go with him to Kuala Lumpur to meet her at the airport, although the journey back to Johor Bahru on the train was a little tense. We could not communicate openly in her father's presence.

Finally, early the following year, I plucked up the courage to approach Umi's father, and told him I wanted to marry her.

I thought he would be furious. In fact, he was not. He did not want us to get married immediately. His elder daughter had gone to university. He asked me to wait till she graduated. Umi was impatient, unwilling to carry on as we were for four more years. My own mother was adamant – Umi's family had treated me well and I must not let them down. 'You have already waited 12 years – you will just have to wait another four!' So we did.

Finally, in December 1958, the wedding took place – in fact, two weddings. Umi's sister got married at the same time. And Umi and I have been together ever since.

THE REALITIES OF LIFE IN POSTWAR SINGAPORE

After I qualified as a social worker, I came face to face
with the problems of poverty and disease faced by many people
in Singapore and Malaya in the period after World War II.
That is the benchmark against which I measure the progress
we have made since.

A few months after receiving my social work diploma at the University of Malaya, I got a job. In February 1955 I started work as an almoner, a medical social worker. For the first few months I worked at the outpatient department at the General Hospital at Outram (now Singapore General Hospital); and at the tuberculosis clinic at Tan Tock Seng Hospital. In those days, tuberculosis, a very dangerous bacterial infection of the lungs, was much more common than it is now. Poor nutrition and unhealthy housing conditions were contributing factors. Many people were living in stressful, overcrowded conditions where disease could spread very easily. Sometimes their problems were psychological. Among the most difficult tasks was talking to people whose illness was incurable and who had nowhere to go on discharge from hospital.

Because the hospitals were so full, there was great pressure to keep the flow of patients moving and clear the beds. But many people had nowhere to go. Many Chinese and Indians had come to Singapore when they were very young. They had lost contact with their families, back at their places of origin. Now they might have contracted tuberculosis, or be bedridden after a stroke. Many of the poorer Indians were living in overcrowded quarters around Serangoon Road. Poorer Chinese were also lodging in shophouses divided into tiny cubicles, or in attap houses. Some of them went for help to their clan associations, where they could only rest during the day, have a wash and have tea – but they had to find somewhere else to sleep at night, often in the five-foot ways.

After a few months I was asked to go to work at some of the rural medical clinics. There were clinics at Bukit Panjang, Bukit Timah 7th Mile and Paya Lebar. Doctors were in short supply. For example, in the outpatient clinic at Bukit Panjang there were one doctor, two nurses and one person dispensing medicines – they had to cover a large area stretching all the way up from Bukit Timah Road as far as Woodlands, and westward as far as Lim Chu Kang and Ama Keng. Some clinics, such as the ones at Katong or Changi, had no doctors at all. If you wanted to see a doctor and did not want to pay for your treatment (or couldn't afford to) you generally had to find your way into town. Fortunately there was a lively community spirit in the kampongs and there was usually a neighbour willing to accompany you.

I used to travel around many of these outlying areas where the landscape today has been changed by the

I visited patients in outlying areas to learn more about their problems.

construction of New Towns – places such as Lim Chu Kang, Choa Chu Kang and Punggol. I would go into the houses and talk to the patients about their problems. I found it much more rewarding than working in the hospital, where I often sensed that some doctors regarded my involvement as interference.

This was my first real contact with rural life in Singapore. Many of the villages I went to were connected to vegetable, pig and poultry farms. There were coconut trees (falling coconuts were a real danger), and wooden houses with attap roofs, all clustered together. Some people were keeping poultry and there were always children playing around. There was certainly poverty, but the atmosphere among the villagers was one of contentment.

Occasionally I came across people I did not expect to find. I had a suspicion that some left-wing political agitators were using the kampongs as places where they could keep a low profile, unnoticed by the authorities. Once, I had to go to a house at Lim Chu Kang. Houses were often divided up into small cubicles, and one of the cubicles was rented out to someone who claimed to be a student. When I went to see him, I found a man who was as old as I was, or even older – at least 30. Supposedly he was studying at Nanyang University, and I asked him what his subject was. He mumbled something, but he was very evasive. Although he may have been involved in student politics, I do not believe he was a student.

My life as an almoner was an important learning experience. It is easy to forget how serious the social problems were in Singapore in the 1950s, in some ways worse than on the peninsula, in what is now Malaysia. There, if they couldn't get work, people could at least go back to their villages and help

on the farms. There was a community to which they could turn. Singapore had become desperately overcrowded during the years after World War II, and people had nowhere else to go. Poverty had become a much tougher problem. To make matters worse, many heads of families had been killed by the Japanese, creating difficulties for the wives and children who survived.

Looking on the brighter side, this meant that after society had been disrupted by the war, we had the opportunity to start anew. We had gained experience solving problems without the British and with little interference from the Japanese. Because things were in such a bad state, we were able to approach our economic and social problems with fresh and radical ideas, rebuilding with fewer obstacles in the way.

The mobile clinic and dispensary helped villagers who could not travel to a doctor in town.

A SUMMONS FROM
DAVID MARSHALL

Late in 1955, when I was working as a medical social worker,
the Chief Minister David Marshall summoned me to his office.
It was months before our conversation led to anything, but it brought
about one of the most significant steps forward in my career.
I was about to enter a new world.

The telephone rang. On the line was the office of the Chief Minister, David Marshall. I was to drop everything, and go to the Fullerton Building, where he was working that day. I had never met Marshall in person, and I was apprehensive.

Marshall had a habit of holding 'Meet the People' sessions in front of the press. He would make civil servants respond on the spot to complaints from the public. Had I done something wrong? Had someone complained?

As I entered his office, the Chief Minister was sitting in a swivel chair, behind a large table. Before I could say anything he came to the point. He said that a 'Seamen's Advisor', an Englishman by the name of T.A. White, would be leaving. He asked if I would take over from White when the time came for him to leave. I said I would be happy to do so if the Chief Minister wanted me to. Marshall called a British civil service officer, named Fraser, said that he had spoken to me, and told him to see to my appointment. He thanked me, and said I could go. That was the end of the conversation. More than ten years went by before I was to meet Marshall again.

Outside the room, I asked Fraser why the Chief Minister had chosen me. My only relevant experience, if any, was a thesis I had written for the Social Studies diploma course at the University of Malaya, on 'The nature and extent of work done in Singapore for the welfare of merchant seamen'. 'Search me,' Fraser said.

Months went by. I heard nothing. Marshall resigned as Chief Minister and was replaced by Lim Yew Hock. But during the following year, I was told to report to

the 'Master Attendant' in the Marine Department. I was to be an 'Assistant Seamen's Welfare Officer' – no mention of 'Seamen's Advisor', nor any job description. The Master Attendant referred me to his deputy, who in turn referred me to T. A. White, whom Marshall had mentioned earlier.

White explained that his job was to be split into two. He told me that a civil servant, by the name of Goh Sin Tub, was being transferred from the Ministry of Labour to be a Seamen's Industrial Relations Officer, reporting to the Ministry of Commerce and Industry. He was to deal with 'industrial relations'; I was to deal with 'seamen's welfare'. T. A. White had helped set up a number of trade unions for local seamen, which could then negotiate a collective agreement with the shipping companies. These unions were to work with Goh, following White's departure. He did not say what 'seamen's welfare' entailed.

David Marshall, sitting at a table, asked if I would serve as a Seamen's Advisor.

On the industrial relations front, there were other unions, outside the collective agreement in force at the time. They were not well run. For example, the Indo-Malay-Pakistani Seamen's Union was led by a man called M.A. Majid. According to White, it was a one-man show with no proper membership other than a loose group of seafarers exploited at the whim of one individual, Majid himself. He handled anything involving Indian seamen, including those working on the tramp steamers plying between Calcutta and Singapore, as well as large numbers of men originating from Goa and working in the catering role. He was physically impressive, with a mop of greying hair; he was also notorious for trying to start legal cases, and neither shipowners nor officials would deal with him if they could possibly help it.

I reported for work at the Fullerton Building. Exactly what I should be doing was not clear. I was starting a new career in a new field, in a role that no one could clearly define – not my superiors in the Marine Department, nor the seafarers whose interests I was supposed to be concerned about, nor the shipowners who employed them.

To begin with, Goh and I tried to stick to our allotted areas of responsibility – 'industrial relations' and 'seamen's welfare' respectively. We soon realised that reality was not so clear-cut – the two were inter-related, and overlapped. Goh proposed, and I agreed, that he should deal with trade union matters; and I should deal with individual seamen and their problems.

During my six-year stint as a Seamen's Welfare Officer, I saw many injustices, and many men without work in desperate circumstances. I learned that in cases of dispute or distress, pointing to the 'contract' was often not enough. There was a human angle. Suffering often extended beyond the individual seamen to their families. It was painful to witness, and still haunts me to this day. I have described some of my experiences while on this job in greater depth in my book *Why Am I Here?*

LIFE ON THE WATERFRONT

*In my work as a Seamen's Welfare Officer, I learned about
the difficulties seafarers faced in their dealings with employers,
and the desperate conditions many of them put up with during
their time ashore, while unemployed.*

Before reclamation of the land on which Marina Bay Sands now stands, Collyer Quay faced the open sea. It was the commercial heart of the city. Here and in Raffles Place nearby were the big banks and commercial firms, as well as the Marine Department, where I worked. The department managed the port, among other things.

Our offices were in the Fullerton Building, which at that time housed the General Post Office. Above the post office were several government departments. I worked in a room on the second floor, with a view away from the sea.

The main buzz of the waterfront was at Clifford Pier. It was a social centre, a meeting place 24 hours a day for seamen looking for work. It was filled with porters, hawkers, food- and drink-sellers, shipping agents, passengers, crews of all nationalities, traders, stevedores, ship chandlers, and officials of all kinds. Small boats shuttled back and forth from the pier carrying food and

A boarding house in Chinatown — many people shared a common space.

other supplies to ships anchored near the breakwater. At that time most people travelling to Singapore still came by sea. The big ships would anchor offshore, and launches would ply between them and the pier, where passengers would finally disembark.

Large cargo ships often unloaded at the Tanjong Pagar wharves, but sometimes their loads were transferred on to lighters at sea which would carry them into the Singapore River. Then, running up and down precarious planks, coolies, as labourers were often called then, would shift the cargo item by item into storage warehouses along the banks of the Singapore River known as godowns, or on to lorries. They carried rubber, timber, cement, coal, grain and other produce – it was a back-breaking life.

Boat Quay was lined with these wooden-hulled lighters, moored in rows. You can see them in many old photographs and postcards. At that time, the mid-1950s, there were still over 500 of them operating out of the Singapore River, the Rochor Canal and Telok Ayer Basin. They were crewed mostly by casually employed men from southeast China, speaking Hokkien and Teochew. They weren't motorised – they were towed by motor launches acting as tugs, and manoeuvred into their berths with poles. The launches were mostly crewed by Malays and Boyanese.

The streets in Chinatown were a bustle of activity.

My job title was 'Seamen's Welfare Officer'. Who were my clients?

Most seamen working out of Singapore had no local families or any permanent home here. Some Hainanese had homes in far-flung places in Singapore such as Kampong Chai Chee, near Changi. However, they always gave addresses in the Hainanese part of town where the *kongsi* (clan associations) were – Middle Road,

Liang Seah Street, Bain Street. A *kongsi* was a useful base when the men were between jobs. The Hainanese were mainly stewards and cooks on regional and ocean-going ships, although some of the younger ones did engine-related work on smaller vessels. Most of the seafarers in the engine rooms were Cantonese. Those in the deck department were mostly Hockchew, from Fuzhou, north of Guangzhou on the Chinese coast. They had no families, but used boarding houses around Tanjong Pagar, in Tras Street, Cheng Cheok Street, and the like.

Malay seamen came mostly from the coastal areas of Malacca, although there were some of Boyanese or other Indonesian origin. They were deck hands. Only a few had homes and families in Singapore – the rest found accommodation in Boyanese pondoks, simple houses with partitioned rooms in the Jalan Besar area.

There were some Pakistani nationals from what is now Bangladesh, who did similar-jobs on coal-burning ships. Without local homes of their own, they were identified with particular boarding houses linked to their places of origin, such as Chittagong, Naokhali and Sylhet. These were mostly in the Serangoon Road area around Norris Road and Rangoon Road.

Conditions in the boarding houses were appalling, as they were throughout much of overcrowded Chinatown and other older parts of the city at the time. Men slept on communal wooden platforms a metre or so above floor level, and covered with straw mats or linoleum. Ropes were slung overhead for drying clothes. The occupants had to cook their own food.

Seafarers constantly faced periods of unemployment. As a result, many of them were permanently in debt to the boarding-house owners.

The services of a Welfare Officer, such as myself, were constantly in demand.

DISPUTES ON BOARD SHIP

My work as Seamen's Welfare Officer occasionally took me into tense situations overseas. I learned to assess the people involved and the nature of their disagreements. I had to make decisions on the spot, use some ingenuity, and take responsibility for the outcome.

The pilgrim ship *Anshun* was docked in Karachi. Its routine was to take Muslim devotees from Southeast Asia to Jeddah for the Haj, and on the return leg pick up Pakistani soldiers and their families in Karachi, and drop them off in East Pakistan (now Bangladesh), before returning to Singapore. Some soldiers had accused an unidentified Malay crew member of molesting one of their womenfolk. There was a real danger that the culprit, if identified, might be murdered. The soldiers would not let the ship sail on until they felt justice had been done. The ship's master let some of them on board, accompanied by the women concerned, to search for the guilty. The alleged victim could not identify anyone – one reason was that all the women were in *purdah*, and they could not clearly make out the seamen's faces in the poor light below deck.

Deadlock. I was asked to sort out the situation, with the help of the local authorities and a member of Singapore's Muslim Advisory Board, himself a Pakistani.

I discovered that the sailors had been giving out water and rice to the passengers. One of them had taken the hand of one of the ladies. The colour of her skin was so fair, he said, that he could not resist the temptation, hoping just to see her face. Unfortunately for him, she let out such a yell that pandemonium erupted. He and some other crew members dashed ashore, and waited for the Pakistanis' anger to die down.

The only solution I could think of was to discharge the culprit and anyone else who wanted to leave the ship, and transport them back to Singapore on another vessel. We had to get the guilty man away as part of a group so he could not be identified. At the same time we gave the soldiers another day to search the ship,

after which it would depart. The soldiers grudgingly agreed, threatening to kill the culprit if they ever found him. Finally the ship sailed.

The other occasion involved a cruise ship of the Nederland Line, the *Johan van Oldenbarnevelt*, which had docked at Lima, in Peru.

The shipping line was employing Singapore catering crew on most of their ships, mainly as stewards and cabin boys. Typically, there were 300–400 of our seamen on each vessel. Passengers had complained of unruly crew behaviour. Service standards had dropped. There was no discipline and passengers felt threatened. The ship's master wanted to discharge the whole Singapore contingent of a few hundred. There was a danger that this action might extend to all the Singapore crew in the company's cruise-ship fleet. This would have been a disaster at a time of high youth unemployment and would have played into the hands of left-wing agitators.

The company agreed that I should fly out to the ship. Their senior crew manager in Holland would do the same. In those days aircraft had a shorter range than they have today, and I had to land at Hong Kong, Tokyo, Honolulu, Los Angeles and Miami! By the time I got to Lima, I was so tired I fell asleep in the immigration queue, standing up.

We arranged for the ship to set sail for its next port of call, Miami. The master and chief steward told me that the goings-on in the dining room amounted to hooliganism. Tablecloths had been pulled away while passengers – children included – were still eating, splashing food over clothing. There was an atmosphere of fear among the older catering staff. A group of about six crew members seemed to be doing no work at all, and were behaving like fare-paying passengers. Each time the ship reached a port, they would go ashore like tourists, without formal leave or doing their share of shipboard duties. Other members of the crew would 'voluntarily' stand in for them.

They were secret society members. They held gambling sessions at the end of each working day. Every crew member was forced to play for cash stakes. The money came from tips given by passengers. They would disrupt the work of anyone who refused to co-operate – this explained the tablecloth incidents. Defiance was dealt with using physical violence and the threat of being thrown overboard – such things could happen near the stern of the ship unnoticed by the ship's watch-keepers. The

men were armed with knuckle-dusters and blackjacks, and, I was told, had hidden revolvers in the lifeboats.

One man whom I knew before advised me not to raise the matter at a general crew meeting, as the ringleaders would be present, and there had been threats of intimidation.

I made a plan. I would interview each crew member, while the ship sailed through the Panama Canal, and on via Miami to New York. From the interviews I got a clear picture of the goings-on, and the particulars of the ringleaders. Before we reached Miami, the master cabled the ship's agents in New York, asking the police and customs to board the vessel. They would search the ship, including the lifeboats. Having (we hoped) discovered the weapons, the master and the officials would ask the crew to own up.

We did not expect anyone to confess, and no one did. While this performance was taking place on arrival in New York, no crew members were allowed to leave

The unruly behaviour of some of the crew shocked and frightened the passengers.

the ship without permission. Then, the master exercised his right to discharge a number of men, including the troublemakers, whom I had identified, plus a few others who wanted to go for their own reasons. Order was thus restored, and I flew back to Singapore.

The story did not quite end there. The company's agents in Singapore wanted the men concerned to be de-registered. This would have taken months, as the the ship's master would have had to give his account of the events. He was not inclined to pursue the matter, and it was decided, on my recommendation, not to impose further penalties, treating the men as if they had signed off 'by mutual consent'.

A few weeks later, one of the men responsible for the disruption called at my office. With his finger round his belt, he asked why I had advised the master to discharge him. I said that the master had acted within his rights. He was not satisfied and left the office, telling me in Malay to 'be careful'. A seaman who had seen this exchange told me to be on my guard, as I might not have noticed the man's secret-society connection. The finger around the belt was a sign that he belonged to the powerful '08' society.

Chinese secret societies were a fact of life at that time. There were a few Malay gangs, too, although on a smaller scale. The gangs never explicitly threatened me, although occasionally a meek-looking seaman would turn up in my office accompanied by an obvious strong-arm type. We had to take such things in our stride.

A MEETING WITH GOH KENG SWEE

At various times in my career I have been asked to take up posts without any clear job description. One of these requests led me into the world of trade unions, and my first working relationship with one of the founding fathers of modern Singapore. This led to both a change of career, and a chance to promote the long-term interests of the country's workers.

In December 1961 I had a call from Dr Goh Keng Swee, asking me to come to his office.

Dr Goh had a brilliant mind – he had earned a first-class honours degree at the London School of Economics and a University of London doctorate in economics. He was one of the pioneer members of the People's Action Party (PAP), and became party vice chairman in 1959, when the Secretary-General was Lee Kuan Yew, whom Goh had got to know in London. In that year, Goh was elected to the Legislative Assembly, and joined Lee's government as Minister for Finance, with responsibility for driving forward Singapore's economic development.

The civil service had already informed me that I was to be transferred into a new job. I was to be assistant director of the 'Labour Research Unit' (LRU). I had not heard of this body; nor, it seemed, had anyone else. It did not seem to exist officially. In an effort to find out more information, I had written to the Ministry of Finance. This request had led to the meeting with Dr Goh.

After sitting me down, he came to the point. He told me about the political struggle with the pro-communist left, not only at the

Dr Goh Keng Swee.

Dr Goh would visit development sites personally to monitor progress.

political level, but also within the trade union movement. The government was trying to win workers over, persuading them to give up their leftist allegiances. But they had to be assisted in their handling of disputes with their employers. He said this was only the first step in a long-term campaign – having got union members 'on its side', the government had to make sure that they were looked after. This was to be the job of the LRU, set up for the purpose. Dr Goh understood my puzzlement. He explained: 'We knew of the work you are doing and your sympathies for workers. We thought it natural to include you in the team, and believed you would agree.'

Dr Goh told me that a 'life and death' struggle was taking place, that could go either way if we were not careful. He referred to the communist habit of wiping out those who opposed them. He said, 'If they win, you and I will be put on the Padang and shot.'

He was not joking. We both remembered the way the communists had behaved at the end of World War II. I knew how the Malayan People's Anti-Japanese Army had punished those who had refused to co-operate or align themselves with them. I had heard reports of their atrocities, and I knew how serious the situation was.

So I told Dr Goh that I would go to the LRU as he had requested, and do my best to help. I was to be 'Assistant Director' (an inflated title for a job in a newly established organisation about which little was known), and in effect, a hands-on activist for the trade union movement. The unit officially came into existence in December 1962, with one of my student colleagues from the University of Malaya, Hsu Tse-Kwang, as head. We were allocated two rooms in a corner of the National Museum building, at the end closest to the old National Library. We had to construct our own office space.

Our job was to assist the trade union movement. But how? That was for us to work out.

And so my full-time commitment to the trade union movement in Singapore began. This was the first of several times in my career when I found myself working with Dr Goh, who played a key role in shaping the political, economic and military development of Singapore at a critical time. My brief was vague. We in the LRU had to define it as we went along, handling disputes as they arose.

LABOUR UNREST AND THE COMMUNIST THREAT

Singapore's survival has always depended on growth through economic development. For 20 years after the end of World War II, for political reasons, communist sympathisers did their best to sabotage it.

Trade unions began to spring up in Singapore immediately after World War II. The Malayan Communist Party (MCP), backers of the MPAJA, had emerged from the war in a strong position, and could now operate openly. During the British Military Administration and the civil administration that followed, strikes and disruption happened almost daily, in Singapore and in towns throughout Malaya. The communists were behind much of the chaos.

By infiltrating trade unions, the communists were tapping into public discontent caused by economic hardship. By sabotaging the economy they hoped to create conditions favourable to a communist takeover. Then, in 1948, a communist-led insurgency and attempted insurrection in Malaya led to the declaration of the Emergency, and the MCP was banned. Industrial calm was restored for a time.

In the early 1950s, industrial unrest began to resume in Singapore. This coincided with unrest among Chinese middle-school students. They were supposedly trying to protect Chinese education, but their underlying mission was to confront the colonial government and create conditions favourable to revolution. During this time, I was at university. I remember many cases of unrest similar to events immediately after the war ended, particularly in the factories around Bukit Timah Road. In 1955, for example, there were nearly 300 strikes and 946,000 man-days lost, with a devastating impact on the economy.

The 1950s and 1960s saw changes in the way trade unions were organised. In 1951, the government backed the formation of the Singapore Trades Union Congress (STUC). Among those involved was Lim Yew Hock, who later became Chief Minister.

In 1954, the People's Action Party (PAP) was formed, with Lee Kuan Yew as Secretary-General. Among the PAP's over-riding aims were the end of colonial rule, and the unification of Singapore with Malaya. At that stage Lee saw working with the communists as a practical necessity.

Following communist-inspired riots in 1956, several top trade union leaders associated with the union movement were detained. In 1957, the pro-communists tried to take control of both the PAP and the STUC. In the elections for the PAP's 12-member central committee, six pro-communist candidates were voted in. The government, now led by Lim Yew Hock, decided to stop the communists in their tracks, and detained a number of political and trade union figures regarded as a threat to national security. A few were exiled to China. The group included five of the six new communist members of the PAP committee.

In May 1959, the first general election under the Rendel Constitution paved the way for Singapore to attain self-governing status, in effect a 'half-way house' on the way to full independence. Although the PAP gained 43 of the 51 seats, it insisted on the release of eight of its communist-inclined top leaders who were in detention, before it would form a government. The British government consented, and so the group, which included Devan Nair (later Secretary-General of the NTUC), walked free, having signed a document pledging their support for the PAP's commitment to independence through merger with Malaya to form Malaysia. Later, Devan Nair was the only one of the signatories to honour that pledge.

At a May Day Rally in 1960 there came the announcement of the formation of a new trade union body, the Trade Union Congress (TUC), backed by the PAP. For a time, both pro-communists and non-communists in the PAP and TUC seemed to be working well together, but behind closed doors, there were heated arguments over Singapore's future, and particularly over unification with Malaya. The communists feared that they would come under pressure from the Federal government in Malaya, which had already spent years confronting communists during the Emergency.

In 1961, tensions over the merger plans led to an open split in both the PAP and the trade union movement. That was the start of an epic battle for the allegiance of Singapore's workers as well. It was to set the direction of the nation's politics for years to come.

THE BIG SPLIT IN THE PAP

*In the early 1960s the tensions between communists and
non-communists in politics and the trade union world broke out
into the open. The situation required firm government action,
which laid the foundations for the stability enjoyed
by Singapore today.*

The tensions within the trade union movement and the People's Action Party (PAP) reached breaking point in 1961, when a by-election was held at Anson. Six leftist members of the Trade Union Congress (TUC) secretariat said they would back the PAP candidate, Mahmud Awang, only if the government called off negotiations for merger with Malaya, scrapped security laws and released all political detainees.

The government refused. The anti-merger, pro-communist faction urged their supporters to back David Marshall, the former Chief Minister standing as a candidate for the Workers' Party, which he had founded in 1957. It did not seem to matter that they had reviled Marshall when he was in power, or that Mahmud Awang was president of the TUC.

Marshall narrowly won the election. This helped to focus the minds of the leadership of the Federation of Malaya, who had to consider more seriously the possibility of communist political dominance of Singapore. Prime Minister Tungku Abdul Rahman, hitherto reluctant to agree to merger, now proposed an association of states that would include not only the Federation of Malaya and Singapore, but also Sarawak, British North Borneo as it then was (now Sabah), and Brunei.

Tensions in the PAP reached breaking point. In July 1961, Lee Kuan Yew successfully demanded a vote of confidence on the merger issue from the Legislative Assembly, following which six rebel assemblymen were expelled from the PAP, together with more than 20 local officials. The rebels went on to form a new and separate political party, the Barisan Sosialis, led by Lim Chin Siong. Many PAP branches switched sides.

The labour movement was similarly split. The Secretary-General of the TUC was G. Kandasamy, a non-communist. He urged the government to dissolve the TUC, which they did. The pro-communists went on to form the Singapore Association of Trade Unions (SATU), with Lim Chin Siong at the helm. The non-communists went on to set up a 14-member preparatory committee to form a new trade union umbrella body that was to become known as the National Trades Union Congress (NTUC). Kandasamy was Deputy Secretary-General. The Secretary-General was Devan Nair, who was to play a central role in Singapore's trade union movement, including the development of NTUC, and later went on to become the Republic of Singapore's third president.

The rivalry between SATU and NTUC had catastrophic consequences, with increased militancy on both sides, the main difference between them being that the NTUC-affiliated unions did not bring politics into their industrial disputes. The year 1961 saw more than 410,800 man-days lost to strikes, compared to 26,587 in 1959, the year when the PAP had first come to power.

The reality was that the pro-communist unions were sacrificing workers to a cause which the workers had not chosen — the road to communist revolution. Whereas in the 1950s the pro-communists made some show of wanting industrial peace, the 1960s saw them pressuring unions to avoid any attempts at arbitration and reconciliation. They fanned the flames of bitterness and hatred among workers who at the beginning just wanted better wages and working conditions. They used violence, for example, intimidating non-striking workers by burning them with cigarette butts, and beating up members of management. They tried to provoke violence on the part of the authorities.

They got off to a flying start. Just as one PAP branch after another defected to the Barisan Sosialis, so one trade union after another defected to SATU. Soon SATU had the support of 82 unions, including seven out of every ten Chinese-dominated industrial unions. Left-wing dominance stretched over most of the economy, including manufacturing and commercial firms, public transport, the port and the naval base. The number of unions remaining affiliated to NTUC was small by comparison.

The people of Singapore subsequently, in 1962, voted in a referendum in favour of merger with Malaya along the lines proposed by the PAP. Neverthess the pro-communists did everything possible to scuttle the formation of Malaysia. To prevent them from inciting more violence, in February 1963 the British, through the Internal Security Council, which they established at the time of self-government, launched Operation Cold Store, detaining many of the communist leaders.

SATU did not last for long. In October 1963, it called a three-day general strike by Singapore workers to protest against moves by the government to de-register seven of the main SATU-affiliated unions. The public response was poor. The strike folded after just one day, and the seven unions were later dissolved. A nail was driven into SATU's coffin when its application for formal registration was rejected, on the grounds that it was serving unlawful purposes inconsistent with its own rules.

It was not long before those unions still loyal to SATU distanced themselves from it, and moved into the NTUC fold. NTUC became the dominant umbrella body for trade unionism in Singapore, and has remained so ever since.

From this turbulent time I draw the lesson that one has to stand up to threats and intimidation with courage and determination, particularly when they are designed to thwart efforts to reach some national objective. It is that experience that I described more fully in my book *Winning Against the Odds*.

THE LRU:
HELPING RESOLVE DISPUTES AND DIFFERENCES IN THE WORKPLACE

My work with the Labour Research Unit gave me first-hand experience of trade union negotiations in Singapore. They were sometimes fierce and emotional. I learned about the problems faced by people at work, and the compromises that have to be made if employees are to be treated fairly while companies remain competitive.

After the split in the People's Action Party (PAP) and the trade union movement, a high-level discussion took place between Prime Minister Lee Kuan Yew, Finance Minister Goh Keng Swee, and National Trades Union Congress (NTUC) Secretary-General Devan Nair. They agreed that official back-up was needed for unions that had escaped communist domination. Otherwise there was a danger that they might drift back into the clutches of the left. This was the thinking behind the creation of the Labour Research Unit (LRU).

When I started work at the LRU, initially as Assistant Director (later I became Director), neither I nor my colleagues had much idea of what our role should be. We knew that we were supposed to 'assist' the trade unions, but we were not told how. So we made up our job descriptions as we went along.

One of our main roles was to help trade unions negotiate wage agreements or grievance procedures, especially those that had been disrupted following the split within the union movement. Sometimes I almost found myself playing the role of unionist. Some of the union leaders did not speak good English. Even when they did, they tended to thump tables and issue threats, which did their cause no good. Some union leaders were so convinced of the rightness of their case that they refused our advice. Not every union official was taking his role seriously – some of them used their role as an opportunity just to throw their weight around in the workplace, and be absent from their post during working hours.

Particularly in the new industries on the Jurong Industrial Estate, there were frequent arguments about 'recognition' – deciding which union a company would recognise as the representative of its workforce. The labour ministry was often called in to adjudicate. The ministry would hold a secret ballot, in which each worker would cast a vote privately, free of pressure from other people. This was a move away from the traditional 'show of hands', in which everyone could see how everyone else was voting, and intimidation was common. Occasionally these arguments brought threats of strong-arm tactics, or even acid attacks.

By being patient, spending time with our trade union clients, however frustrating the experience sometimes was, we were able to build up relationships, and promote effective negotiating practices. We also built up first-hand information on developments within the union movement and at the workplace.

For me, these experiences were an education. During my time with the LRU, I was able to build on my earlier expertise in handling the grievances of seamen. I honed my negotiating skills, something that proved useful later in my career. I practised my ability to listen.

This was a time when Dr Goh Keng Swee, on behalf of the government, was trying to attract foreign companies to set up industrial plants in Singapore. The case of Jurong Shipyard is one example. It was a joint venture between a Japanese company and the Economic Development Board (EDB). We needed to establish a fair and efficient wage structure. Neither the company's management nor their own in-house union in Japan initially welcomed the LRU's involvement. In my search for a model agreement, I found one signed by a local British-owned engineering company. It had a flexible wage structure based on levels of skill, as well as rewards for years of service and productivity. After a visit to the company's head office in Japan, we were able to get the proposed terms agreed by all those involved.

There were several such cases in which we had to strike a balance between the need for a company to be profitable (why else would anyone invest in Singapore?) and the need to improve local working conditions. With the coming of multinationals and modern manufacturing methods came also properly regulated working conditions and terms of employment. The age of the sweatshop was past.

FOREIGN AFFAIRS

After I had been working with the trade union movement for some time, when Independence came I was transferred to a key government ministry — although at that time I had very little relevant experience, and the ministry itself was 'learning on the job'.

In December 1965, independent Singapore was only four months old. That month, I started work as an 'Assistant Secretary' (a junior civil servant) in the political division of the newly established Ministry of Foreign Affairs (MFA).

I reported for work. The ministry was so new that construction of its offices had not yet been finished. We occupied part of an upper floor in the west wing of City Hall. I was given a little cubicle with a view into the general office. More senior people, including the Minister and the Permanent Secretary, had windows overlooking the Padang, but even their accommodation was modest.

It was several months before the political division was fully up and running. At first we made up our processes and procedures day by day. In mid-1966, the Permanent Secretary returned from the United Nations (UN) in New York, where Singapore had secured admission as a member. After that, our work was better organised, with a chain of command. At the top we had the Permanent Secretary as the civil service head, and the Minister as the political master.

What was Singapore's foreign policy? When I asked the Foreign Minister, S. Rajaratnam, what principles I was supposed to follow in dealing with matters that came to me, his reply was: 'Don't worry, it will come naturally.' Throughout my career I have had to improvise, to make up my job description as I went along. My job at MFA was no exception. I was 41 years old, with no first-hand diplomatic experience, apart from some international trade union activities. Only two of the officials in the division had experience in foreign relations. So we reacted to day-to-day developments using our common sense. The Permanent Secretary was in no better a position than the rest of us.

Fortunately the Minister, Rajaratnam, was approachable, and would give us guidance when, for example, important foreign embassies would ask us to clarify things that Prime Minister Lee Kuan Yew had said to the foreign press. He and other leaders made many speeches which set out Singapore's sympathies with other countries seeking independence. The leaders also explained why they had sought merger with Malaysia – and why the merger had come unstuck. They dwelt at length on the vulnerabilities of Singapore, a newly independent state. Security was a primary area of concern. Australia, New Zealand and Britain all had troops in Singapore, and it was repeatedly explained to them why their continued presence was in their own interests.

Rajaratnam's speeches were particularly helpful. At the UN General Assembly in 1965, explaining Singapore's commitment to non-alignment, he said: 'We have no wish to interfere in the affairs of other countries or tell them how they should order their life. In return we ask other countries to be friendly with us even if they do not like the way we do things in our own country. ... This is why we do not wish to be drawn into alliances dedicated to imposing our way of life on other countries. Friendship between two countries should not be conditional on the acceptance of common ideologies, common friends and common foes.'

The main thrust in our foreign relations was to cultivate as many permanent friends as possible. The ministry initially focused its attention on our closest neighbours, including Malaysia, Indonesia and Thailand, and on developments in the Vietnam War. Kuala Lumpur and Jakarta were then our most important diplomatic missions, and took up most of our attention. Our sovereignty and security depended heavily on the way Malaysia, Indonesia and other nations in the region viewed our independence, as we relied on them for trade. As our security was a priority, diplomatic missions were soon established in London, Canberra and Wellington.

Sometimes we made mistakes. For example, we gave a gun salute to a visiting 'Vice-President of the Democratic People's Republic of Korea' (that is, North Korea). As a special envoy of the president we believed he had to be treated as a head of state. It turned out later that this rank was given to anybody whom the Great Leader – Kim Il Sung – sent as a special envoy. There were some 40 of them who had all gone on special missions and had ended up back in Pyongyang. Neither we nor Malaysia knew much about North Korea, and other friendly nations were in a similar position.

It was not easy to build up the right team in the department. Singapore's financial position was not secure, and limits were put on recruitment. Particularly in the first few years, spending money on equipment and services by our overseas

City Hall, formerly home to the Ministry of Foreign Affairs.

missions was over-tightly regulated by the Treasury. However, things improved with time. Looking back, one can appreciate that resources had to be directed to economic development as the main priority.

Australia and New Zealand, together with the United Kingdom and Malaysia, were our partners in the Five Power Defence Arrangements (FPDA), set up in 1971. This agreement meant that 'in the event of any form of armed attack externally organised or supported or the threat of any form of such

I had a cubicle in City Hall, where I was Assistant Secretary in the Political Division of the MFA.

attack against Malaysia and Singapore', the governments of the five countries would consult on measures to deal with it. The presence of FPDA military forces in Singapore reinforced the British presence and strengthened our defences against two major threats: the ongoing communist insurgency in Malaysia, and any possible threat from Indonesia, which had been pursuing Confrontation with Malaysia and Singapore.

The USA was important because it was fighting communist expansion in Vietnam. We counted on the Americans to fill the gap that would be created by a likely British pull-out. Much of our economy had depended on the British presence. The British finally withdrew militarily from the region in the early 1970s, which added to our economic difficulties. Many who worked in the British military establishments lost their jobs, as did domestic helpers working for British families.

When the British withdrew, valuable assets, such as hospitals, naval-base facilities and golf-courses, were returned to the Singapore government. A Bases Economic Conversion Unit was set up so that they could be put to use for Singapore's benefit in a systematic way.

OUR NEAREST NEIGHBOUR, MALAYSIA

*During the years before I joined the Ministry of Foreign Affairs,
Singapore was travelling towards independence,
but the road was bumpy. Among the challenges was our
volatile political relationship with our neighbours
across the Causeway. The relationship has been a key concern
for the Ministry of Foreign Affairs ever since.*

The postwar British Military Administration came to an end in 1946, to be replaced briefly by the Malayan Union. This excluded Singapore. The Malayan Union was replaced in turn by the Federation of Malaya, in 1948. Singapore was not part of either. In my younger days, I identified very much with 'Malaya', and regretted that Singapore was not taking part in political developments on the Malay peninsula. I followed closely the progress of the Federation of Malaya to independence, which it achieved on 31 August 1957.

The day 16 September 1963 saw the formation of the Federation of Malaysia. This time, Singapore was included, as were also Sabah (formerly British North Borneo), and Sarawak. These events were not just something to read about in the newspaper. They had a real impact on my working life in the trade union movement. The Singapore public had voted for joining Malaysia in a referendum the year before, but the communists were dead against it, and did everything they could to sabotage the merger, despite its economic advantages. Communist-inspired disruption of our industries was a daily reality. This was against a broader background in which the Malayan Communist Party was in contact with China. North Vietnam collaborated with China in that endeavour. In South Vietnam the US was getting more deeply involved in war against forces from communist North Vietnam. That year saw Singapore's struggle against opponents of a merger with Malaysia and supporters of Indonesia's Confrontation, which was then at its most intense.

Our membership of the Federation of Malaysia was a hot issue when I was representing the National Trades Union Congress (NTUC) in its efforts to join the Afro-Asian People's Solidarity Organization (AAPSO) in 1964. AAPSO was a grouping of political parties, labour unions and other organisations representing radical elements and liberation movements in Asia and Africa. Many members were suspicious of the very idea of Malaysia, seeing it as a ploy by the British to maintain regional dominance. Indonesia, which had a high profile in the organisation and particularly in its policy-making secretariat, was agressive in its anti-Malaysia campaigning. I was determined to stress Singapore's non-aligned status, and the result of the merger referendum, that had shown overwhelming support by our people. Following a long and winding process of negotiation, NTUC was finally admitted at a meeting in Nicosia in 1966. This reinforced perceptions of Singapore as part of the anti-colonial, non-aligned movement.

Singapore left the Federation of Malaysia on 9 August 1965. I joined the Ministry of Foreign Affairs (MFA) just a few months later, in December. The wounds caused by Separation were still raw on both sides. Nevertheless we saw our ties with Malaysia as important. It was a tense relationship, although we were anxious to make it clear that developments within Malaysia were no longer Singapore's business.

There were frequent bad-tempered exchanges between the foreign ministries of both countries, over, for example, remarks made by Lee Kuan Yew about Malaysia in a television interview in 1965; and over remarks about Singapore published in Malaysian newspapers. According to one Malaysian press report, the Chief Minister of Sarawak had accused Singapore of sending people to Sarawak to carry out subsersive activities and distribute propaganda. We protested and asked for evidence supporting the claim. None ever came. In October 1965, the Malaysians protested when Lee Kuan Yew described Malaysia as a 'medieval feudal society', and commented that 'Maharajas who are of any value are those who work for a living'. They said this was calculated to undermine the constitutional position of the Yang di-Pertuan and the Malay rulers. We reminded Malaysia of similar remarks by Malaysian ministers, and pointed out that undertakings as to non-interference into each other's affairs had to be reciprocal, a two-way street.

In April 1966, we had to protest when Malaysia suddenly started imposing security checks on people entering their territory from Singapore. They announced their intention of introducing full immigration restrictions – supposedly a security measure in response to Indonesian Confrontation, despite the fact that Indonesia had already announced that Confrontation was at an end. Our view was that people-to-people relations and trade were best served by free and unrestricted movement between the two countries.

There were many squabbles of this kind. In 1970 came a spat over the arrest and alleged mistreatment of three Malaysians visiting Singapore. They had, allegedly, been 'questioned and insulted with words against their person, race, and leaders'. When they were released, it was said, the three were forced to have their hair cut within the police station precinct, and pay a dollar each for the privilege. The Singapore version of events gave a different impression. According to an official statement, 'At about 8.30 pm on August 14, a party of CID officers carried out a check at the Orchard Road carpark eating stalls as a result of reports that secret society members were frequenting the stalls. This resulted in the arrest of three Malaysians, as well as four Singaporeans.' As the CID lock-up cells were full, the visitors were detained in the passageway between the charge room and the cells. Next morning they were questioned by detectives. It was true, the official statement said, that the police, as part of their campaign against hippiedom, had lectured them on the undesirability of long hair and apeing the styles and habits of western hippies. After the usual lectures, they were asked whether they would agree to have their hair cut short at a dollar a head. 'They raised no objections,' said the statement, and accordingly 'arrangements were made with the CID barber to have their hair cut short.' Senior politicians on both sides made conciliatory statements, and gradually the fuss died down.

One disagreement had an unexpected consequence. During the merger period, the Singapore and Malayan police forces had been amalgamated. When National Day came around in 1966, they had not yet been totally unscrambled. Singapore wanted the police band to play for the parade. Malaysia refused to give permission. This led Singapore to build up its own bands – school bands, ladies' pipe bands, all sorts – which were featured on important occasions in later years, including National Day.

Despite the stresses and strains in our dealings with Malaysia, my personal relations with Malaysian officials in Singapore and in their foreign ministry were cordial, and sometimes warm and friendly. This was especially so with those who had studied in the University of Malaya in Singapore, and had been my fellow hostelites in Dunearn Road. Co-operation between the police of both countries, and between the security services engaged in fighting communist threats, was unaffected throughout the years.

My engagement with Malaysia was to become even deeper several years later, when I was appointed Singapore's High Commissioner in Kuala Lumpur, but that's another story.

The Malaysians had their hair cut at the police station.

FOUNDING ASEAN

In 1967, five nations formed the Association of Southeast Asian Nations (ASEAN): they were Indonesia, Malaysia, the Philippines, Singapore, and Thailand. I attended the inaugural meeting of foreign ministers in Thailand, and was able to experience international politics at first hand.
Five more countries have joined since.

O n 1 June 1967, the Indonesians were the first to raise with Singapore officially the proposal for the formation of a regional grouping of Southeast Asian nations. There was to be an inaugural meeting of foreign ministers in August, and the Indonesians wanted Singapore to support the project publicly. Singapore had only recently experienced the trauma of Separation from Malaysia. Foreign Minister Rajaratnam said the association should therefore focus on economic, rather than political, aims.

The most divisive problem was the presence of foreign military bases. The non-aligned world (countries without any special affiliations to either the United States or the Soviet Union) was generally hostile to foreign bases, which they saw as a means by which the big powers were trying to dominate the region. This attitude surfaced in the draft of the declaration to be issued after the forthcoming meeting. We saw things differently. There was a British naval base in Singapore, and an Australian air base at Butterworth (in Malaysia), and we regarded these as important pillars of our security. While we did not want the proposed organisation to be seen as an American lackey, we wanted it to focus on economic development, not political or military ganging-up.

On 5–8 August, representatives of the five countries met in Bangkok. When the Indonesians arrived, we expected them to push their military concerns, including joint efforts in fighting subversion, and, of course, the removal of foreign bases. The Malaysians seemed inclined to go along with them – my sense was that they

were indirectly needling Singapore, trying to get us to put up some resistance to the Indonesians, and thus demonstrate that they, the Malaysians, were Indonesia's true friends.

I accompanied Rajaratnam to the informal ministers' meeting. A general discussion took place between the ministers alone, with no one else in the room. Rajaratnam sent for me midway through the meeting. I was to take his files away — he said he was leaving. Just as he reached the door, the Indonesian Foreign Minister, Adam Malik, called out: 'Raja, come back, we can still discuss. Don't do that.' It was clear that the disagreement was about foreign bases.

Rajaratnam spoke to the group of ministers from the door. We were fighting a life-and-death struggle with the communists, he said, one that endangered both us and Malaysia. The presence of the British and Australians was helping us keep the communists at bay. He asked them to imagine what would happen to us without these foreign forces. What would happen if the communists were to

Rajaratnam almost left the room during an informal ASEAN minister's meeting.

win in Vietnam and we were overrun? Ideals are fine, but when our existence is threatened, we must be realistic.

Rajaratnam then rejoined the group and I left the room.

Some time later, around sunset, I was called back in. The ministers had agreed to the importance of having foreign bases until the threat to our security disappeared. I was asked to work with our Thai and Malaysian counterparts to redraft the offending paragraphs. We arrived at a version which reflected the wording in the Afro-Asian 'Cairo Declaration', saying that foreign bases might stay as long as the people of the host country wanted them. The ministers revised the wording in the final declaration.

We worked hard to persuade other delegations to incorporate references to joint projects for economic development. In a final compromise, the ministers agreed to put forward for discussion at future meetings proposals for regional co-operation in such fields as tourism, shipping and fisheries, and the expansion of trade within the region.

Before the draft declaration was formally adopted, there was a last-minute hitch. Tun Razak, the Malaysian Foreign Minister, announced that his Prime Minister, Tungku Abdul Rahman, had promised the Prime Minister of Ceylon (Sri Lanka today) that his country could be admitted as a member. Reluctantly everyone agreed, notwithstanding the definition of Southeast Asia as extending only as far as Burma in the west. They waited for Ceylon's application to arrive. Nothing happened. The clock was ticking, and the Thais were anxious to have the birth of the organisation take place at an auspicious time. Finally, the Thai Foreign Minister called the meeting to order, announced that the ministers had waited long enough, and called the meeting to establish the group formally. He then thanked the Indonesian Foreign Minister Adam Malik for proposing the name 'Association of Southeast Asian Nations' (ASEAN), which was accepted. Thus a new regional organisation was officially born.

Why did the application from Ceylon not arrive? Sri Lanka's former High Commissioner to Singapore, by the name of Gunasingham, told me later that the Prime Minister of Ceylon had come under pressure from the political left within

The ministers representing Indonesia, Malaysia, Thailand, the Philippines and Singapore signed the ASEAN declaration.

his country, and from India, China and the Soviet Union. As he put it, regretfully, 'Sri Lanka's hope of breaking away from its moorings in South Asia and becoming a trading nation with links to South East and East Asian nations as well as to all of littoral Asia was lost.' Their application was shelved, and in later years the internal security situation in the country turned bad.

In his speech at the signing of the declaration, Rajaratnam said this: '... I would like to stress that those who are outside this grouping should not regard this as a grouping against anything, anybody ... So, I would urge people outside the region not to misunderstand this coming together of our five and other South East Asian countries. We want to ensure that ASEAN stands for the interests of ASEAN and therefore for the peace and prosperity of the world. That is all we are interested in.'

Rajaratnam was a very well-read man. Sometimes his language passed over the heads of his audience. Earlier in the proceedings, stressing the need for unity, he had quoted the 18th-century American politician and scientist Benjamin Franklin: 'We must all hang together, or assuredly we will all hang separately.' Afterwards, mystified, a member of one of the other delegations came up to me and asked, 'Why does your Minister say we must hang?'

HOW SINGAPORE REACHED OUT TO THE WORLD

In late 1970 I travelled with Prime Minister Lee Kuan Yew on part of a worldwide tour. We attended an important meeting of 'non-aligned' nations in Zambia. More broadly, the tour gave Singapore an opportunity to build up relations with a number of countries, all very different politically. We wanted to make the world aware of Singapore's status as an independent nation, and our policies on international matters.

When we arrived in Zambia, the Prime Minister was greeted by President Kenneth Kaunda. With Kaunda by his side, Lee Kuan Yew mounted the salutary dais. The Singapore national anthem was played. Then, accompanied by local army and airforce commanders, he inspected a guard-of-honour mounted by the 3rd Battalion, the Zambian Regiment, as a 19-gun salute boomed across the tarmac. Tribal dancers performed as drummers pounded out a traditional African welcome. As we drove from the airport, thousands of Zambians lined the roadside. At the conference many voices were raised in anger towards the developed world. For example, Forbes Burnham, the Prime Minister (and later President) of Guyana proposed that developing countries, with many of the world's mineral resources under their control, should be very aggressive in their demands.

Prime Minister Lee Kuan Yew took a more balanced view. During his speech, he pointed out of the window to the plane that had brought the President of Indonesia. That plane was needed for communications with Jakarta, he said, because the normal phone system was inadequate – a call from Lusaka would have to go through Dar es Salaam, Nairobi, London and then to Singapore, before getting to Indonesia. His point was that technology was important in the modern era, and that the conference should recognise that the developed and developing worlds depended on each other. The developing world might have all the resources, but still needed technology to extract them profitably.

One head of state from Central Africa looked particularly impressive, wearing a military uniform with medals all over his chest. I asked one of his delegation who had conferred all these medals. 'Nobody,' was the reply. Apparently he had awarded himself the medals – he had a whole array at home in a cupboard, and regularly changed them around.

This was the first time Singapore had attended such a conference, and the Prime Minister was able to meet the President of Indonesia and representatives of North Korea, among others. The North Koreans wanted to win Singapore's support for their efforts to reunify Korea. The Prime Minister explained Singapore's position, one that it has maintained consistently over many years. It regarded such divisions as internal affairs, and Singapore did not wish to interfere on behalf of either side.

The tour was a long one. The itinerary included Ceylon (today's Sri Lanka), India, Tanzania, Zambia (as I have mentioned), Egypt, West Germany, the Soviet Union, the Soviet Republic of Georgia, France, the United Kingdom and the United States.

In London we were able to discuss the impact that Britain's military withdrawal from Southeast Asia would have on Singapore and Malaya. They had maintained a very visible presence in Singapore even after independence, and offered some security in the face of the communist threat. The Cold War was still in full force. The British were concerned by the possibility that while in Moscow we might have done some deal with the Soviet Union, offering them facilities for naval ship repair and maintenance. We said we had not, although their fears seemed to persist. A lot of jobs had depended on the British presence, and their departure would be a blow to local employment. This spurred on the Prime Minister's efforts to encourage technologically advanced companies such as Plessey in Britain and Rollei in Germany to invest in Singapore, to help us to improve our workforce's skills and so catch up with developed countries. As he said to the press, Singapore had raised its sights: it was interested in manufacturing sophisticated products with real added value. We wanted to create good jobs, not just the low-skilled jobs which we had been obliged to accept at a time, after self-government, when unemployment was high and investment hard to come by.

Most of the discussions on the tour covered the broad sweep of world affairs. But there were moments of human interest too. On the second day of our visit to

Ceylon, Prime Minister Lee had been scheduled to attend a rally at 4.00 pm. After a busy morning in the hot sun, he needed to rest, and after lunch he told me to have him excused from attending. The Ceylonese Chief of Protocol refused to alter a programme that his own Prime Minister had arranged personally. The foreign ministry refused to help on the basis that the programme had been cleared with us before the visit. The clock was ticking, and the Ceylonese Prime Minister, Mrs Bandaranaike, was due to pick us up at her official residence, where we were staying.

I paced up and down the lobby, wondering what to do. The Chief Butler asked me what was wrong. I explained. When Mrs Bandaranaike arrived, he greeted her at the door, and I could see them having a conversation. When she greeted me, she said she had 'got the message' and that she would appear herself at the rally and explain the situation. Later, I asked the butler what he had said. He had asked her which was more important – the rally or the state banquet later? Faced with that question, she had agreed that our Prime Minister could skip the rally in favour of the state banquet.

Of course, this little episode was trivial. But it underlined a point that I have found very important over the years. Lower-ranking staff often have close relations with their bosses and can achieve things that more senior people, without those personal ties, would find difficult. It is important to treat them with respect.

HOW THE WORLD CAME TO SINGAPORE

Any young country, newly independent, would welcome the opportunity to play a part on the world stage. We got such a chance when the Commonwealth Heads of Government Meeting came to Singapore in 1971 for the first time outside London, their traditional home. The conference, under Lee Kuan Yew's chairmanship, went well and without any disruptions, despite the possibility of an African boycott over South African questions. We felt we had arrived internationally.

I had joined the Ministry of Foreign Affairs (MFA) in 1965, just a few weeks after Singapore had left the Federation of Malaysia and became fully independent. Six years later, an event took place that made us feel the country had come of age. That was the Commonwealth Heads of Government Meeting in Singapore.

The former British Empire had almost disappeared, replaced by the 'Commonwealth', in which newly independent, former British colonies played key roles on equal terms with Britain and the old-established members such as Canada and Australia. After 1971, the Commonwealth heads of government no longer met automatically in London. The role of host was to rotate among the members – and in January that year, 31 countries sent their prime ministers to Singapore. From then on, these conferences were known as 'Commonwealth Heads of Government Meetings' (CHOGMs).

Despite the shared Commonwealth background, the members represented a wide variety of political viewpoints. Some governments were committed to non-aligned status (that is: allied with neither the Western powers led by the USA, nor the communist bloc led by the then USSR). Others had signed western-orientated defence treaties. Some states were mixed economies (combining capitalism with public ownership); others were organised on socialist principles. Some were developing; some were already industrialised.

The conference venue was the Singapore Conference Hall. Although its appearance has changed, the building is still there, in Shenton Way. The men and women (mostly men) taking part were seated round a table in the form of a huge oval ring. Chairing the proceedings was our own Prime Minister at the time, Lee Kuan Yew. I was assigned to him as staff officer. My job was to be a link between him and other delegation heads, and also the Commonwealth Secretary-General, Arnold Smith (a Canadian). In the full sessions, Foreign Minister Rajaratnam sat on the Prime Minister's left, and Smith sat on his right.

As the conference went on, I became increasingly involved with helping shape the draft of the joint communiqué. This document is issued at the end of a conference and sums up the final position reached on matters discussed.

The key topics reflected world events at the beginning of the 1970s. The United Kingdom seemed likely to join the European Community, which might affect its traditional trading links with Commonwealth countries, including Singapore. Two African issues were dominating the headlines: the illegal régime in Rhodesia (today's Zimbabwe); and above all a proposed British arms sale to South Africa. This was

The Singapore Conference Hall, venue for important international events.

controversial because South Africa was still run on *apartheid* lines, whereby whites and blacks were kept separate. The former lived privileged lives and the latter suffered intense discrimination.

The South Africa issue stoked up strong passions among African heads of government. Before the conference, some African leaders had threatened to stage a boycott as a protest against the arms sale, or even leave the Commonwealth altogether. It was a tricky situation, and Singapore had to manage it.

When the Prime Minister gave his opening address, he acknowledged that his job was to make sure that all issues could be discussed, and that everyone should get a fair hearing. He accepted that, if consensus was not possible, the countries might have to agree to disagree. The stakes were high. He warned that if Commonwealth leaders could not 'contain our present difficulties over the proposed arms sale, then it is unlikely that the Commonwealth, as at present constituted, can longer endure'.

There were several late-night sessions, and the debate on the South African arms issue went on until about 4.00 am. It took endless patience to bring the conference to a conclusion without a breakdown. The efforts of Arnold Smith and the Commonwealth Secretariat earned our respect.

Government leaders assembled for the Commonwealth Heads of Government meeting in Singapore.

There was one odd coincidence – or was it a coincidence? The British argument for selling maritime defence weaponry to South Africa was based in part on the need to counter increasing Soviet naval activity in the Atlantic and Indian oceans. During the conference a Royal Navy helicopter reported the presence of two Russian warships, followed by a tanker and a supply ship, passing the Raffles lighthouse just south of Singapore and sailing up the Malacca Strait. Was the timing significant? It was several years since a large Russian naval vessel had been seen in Singapore waters.

The conference was not totally hitch-free. One of the few women heads of government at the conference was the Prime Minister of Ceylon (today's Sri Lanka), Mrs Bandaranaike. Every time she tried to speak, the microphone misbehaved. Nothing the technicians could do seemed to make a difference. In the early hours of the morning, after efforts to address the problem after midnight had failed, she had to use the microphone of her neighbour.

Otherwise, the conference went well, and Singapore was able to raise its international profile. We had put ourselves on the map. The chance to host the conference came round again 18 years later, in 1989.

THE KKO CRISIS, AND THE STORMING OF THE EMBASSY

President Sukarno of Indonesia saw Singapore's membership of the Federation of Malaysia as part of a neo-colonial plot, designed to frustrate Indonesia's wish to dominate Southeast Asia. The result was 'Confrontation', an undeclared war in which most of the action was in the border area between Indonesia and Malaysian territory on the island of Borneo, and occasionally in peninsular Malaysia. Singapore did not escape violence completely.

In March 1965, two Indonesian saboteurs set off a bomb in the stairwell of MacDonald House, where at the time HSBC had a large branch on the ground floor (now occupied by Citibank). Three people were killed and more than 30 were injured. In October that year, two Indonesians were put on trial and sentenced to death. As they were said to belong to the KKO, a unit of the Indonesian marines, the episode became known as the KKO crisis.

The Indonesians requested a pardon. The position of S. Rajaratnam, our Minister for Foreign Affairs, was that lives had been lost and the culprits convicted. They could appeal through our judicial system, taking the case to the highest Court of Appeal if they wished. Singapore would accept the outcome, whatever it was, but the law should take its course. The appeal was turned down, and Singapore's President Yusof Ishak rejected a plea for clemency by Indonesia's President Suharto.

The date for the execution was set for 17 October 1968. We were concerned for the safety of our diplomatic staff, as there were fears of riots and the burning of our embassy in Jakarta. The Prime Minister and Foreign Minister were away. Dr Goh Keng Swee, Acting Prime Minister, said, 'We must expect trouble. Be prepared.' Late that afternoon, he told me to go home and get some rest. 'Come back at eight o'clock. By then things may have exploded.'

Indonesia's Information Minister announced that if the two were executed, they would be considered national heroes. That night, we heard from Jakarta that tension was high, but we were assured that our ambassador and staff weren't in serious danger. At 1.00 am on the appointed day, I was monitoring the situation with colleagues in my office at City Hall. The phone rang. It was the Indonesian *chargé d'affaires* (at that stage there was no full ambassador), requesting a meeting. He came to the office and demanded that after the sentence was carried out, the

The MacDonald House bombing caused three deaths and many injuries.

Prime Minister Lee Kuan Yew scattered flowers on the tomb
of the two men executed for the 1965 bombing.

bodies should be handed over to him immediately, so that respects could be paid on Indonesian diplomatic premises. I told him that as far as Singapore was concerned, the two were paying the price for their actions according to the law, and they would be treated like any other criminals. If he wanted to honour them, he could do so, but outside Singapore.

I then received phone calls from local businessmen with ties to Indonesia, urging me to grant the request for fear of serious repercussions otherwise. In the morning I reported the events of the night so far to Dr Goh, who confirmed that I had made the right decision.

At 1.30 am, the situation in Jakarta was clearly getting more dangerous, and our ambassador and staff were advised to move out of the embassy and into the Hotel Indonesia.

Early that morning, the death sentence was carried out. Malay officials from the Ministry of Foreign Affairs, including Ridzwan Dzafir, ensured the proper performance of the Muslim rites, down to the last detail. Every assistance was given to the Indonesian diplomatic representatives in transporting the bodies to Jakarta by

plane. The aircraft took off during the afternoon, carrying the two bodies accompanied by the special envoy and the *chargé d'affaires*. Ridzwan was on duty throughout to ensure that there was no lapse on our part that could be considered irreligious.

In Jakarta, violence broke out. A young mob, several hundred strong, ransacked our embassy, tore down the Singapore flag and dragged it along the ground. They burned furniture and smashed windows. A huge crowd gathered to meet the plane carrying the bodies. The reaction across Indonesia was more widespread and violent than most people expected. Top officials in Jakarta were clearly angry with us, and the view among foreign diplomats there was that we had been a bit rash. Gradually the situation cooled down – the leadership did not prolong the crisis probably because good relations with Singapore were important to Indonesia's economy.

After the KKO crisis our relations with Indonesia went through a difficult period lasting several years. In May 1973, Lee Kuan Yew made his first official visit to Indonesia. Among other gestures, he visited the graves of the two KKO men and scattered flowers. This appeased the Indonesians, and marked the beginning of a new phase in relations between the two countries and their leaders.

Singapore has always considered it very important to build friendships with its neighbours, but developments that affect our security and sovereignty must be met head-on, sentiment notwithstanding. The whole episode demonstrated to me that, although toughness is most effective when combined with diplomacy, it is sometimes essential.

THE BOAT PEOPLE

During the 1960s and the early 1970s, the communist Democratic Republic of Vietnam ('North Vietnam') was fighting a full-scale war with the American-backed Republic of Vietnam ('South Vietnam'). After Saigon, capital of the South, fell to invading forces in 1975, surrounding countries faced a massive refugee problem, as thousands fled the South by boat at great risk. Confronted by the prospect of a huge refugee problem, Singapore had to defend its own interests.

When the defeat of South Vietnam was clearly imminent, many people associated with the government, international companies or foreign diplomatic missions felt vulnerable and were desperate to get out of the country. The better off saw no future for themselves under communism.

We allowed friendly countries to use Singapore as a point from which they could take to their countries those they wanted to get out of Vietnam. The Shell oil company wanted to fly their senior staff out. The Singapore government agreed to let them come here, provided the company moved them on somewhere else quickly, and were responsible for their upkeep when they were here. This arrangement worked well.

We made similar arrangements with the American and British diplomatic representatives. The Americans and others brought out several hundred refugees, whom we housed in tents on St John's Island. We fed them very good meals, consisting of fish, meat and rice, prepared by the SAF kitchens. For some reason, the refugees would not eat – we thought they must be suffering from emotional trauma. Dr Goh Keng Swee had an idea. 'Let's give them some fish sauce,' he said. 'That's something the Vietnamese can't do without.' So we hunted around the shops in Chinatown for a supply of the sauce. It did the trick.

The Americans, British and Australians were slow to move their refugees out. When we complained, a process began, whereby each refugee family was interviewed, so that a decision could be made on their admission to the US, the UK or Australia. The United Nations High Commissioner for Refugees monitored the proceedings.

So what happened? These countries took their pick of the educated and professional people, leaving us with the unskilled farmers, fishermen and odd-job workers and their families. It took the United Nations a long time to repatriate these unfortunate people out of Singapore.

This experience taught us a lesson, and lay behind our subsequent approach to the problem of the 'boat people' in general. These were refugees who had left Vietnam, Laos and Cambodia in terrible circumstances. After the communist victory, supporters of the southern régime were imprisoned and tortured or abused. Thousands were sent to 're-education' camps. A further factor was the war

Marine Police intercepted boats carrying Vietnamese refugees.

between Vietnam and China in 1979, which brought many ethnic Chinese under suspicion by the Vietnam government. Many tried to escape by sea in small boats, facing overcrowding, food shortages and the threat of piracy. Despite their plight, we decided we could not accommodate them, as we could not trust the assurances of foreign governments that they would quickly be found homes elsewhere.

We also had to be open-eyed about what was going on. To some extent, the refugee phenomenon was a racket. After the initial emergency phase, transporting refugees by boat had been turned into a lucrative trade by organised syndicates in Vietnam and elsewhere, which received payments in the form of gold.

We supplied refugee vessels with provisions and asked them to move on. Indonesia and Malaysia were more accommodating, only to find that they too were saddled with the leftovers, after western countries, including Australia and New Zealand, cherry-picked the educated and the talented.

Singapore is a tiny country. We had to take a robust line for our own protection, or we would have been completely overrun. Foreign governments and organisations concerned with refugees criticised us, accusing us of being inhumane or hard-hearted. They conveniently forgot their own failure to live up to earlier undertakings.

It took many years to solve the problem of the boat people. Well into the 1980s, refugees were still turning up at the Bidor Camp in Malaysia and on the Riau Islands in Indonesia. Even in Singapore, a number of refugees who had not been repatriated remained in the Hawkins Road Camp until 27 June 1996, when they were finally sent back to Ho Chi Minh City. The camp closed three days later.

TWO HIJACKS

After the fall of Saigon to communist forces in 1975, many people in South Vietnam were desperate to escape the country. We had to deal with two hijacking incidents. Although the man behind one of them showed great resourcefulness, we did not condone acts of this kind.

I got a phone call one night, saying that a pilot was threatening to crash-land a military transport aircraft at Paya Lebar Airport, pleading shortage of fuel. This was our international airport – the one at Changi had not yet been built. I rushed to the scene. By the time I arrived, the plane had landed. The pilot was an impressive military type, accompanied by a group of family members and other people, some of them rather scruffy.

The pilot asked for political asylum for himself and his family. He told us that he was a North Vietnamese fighter pilot, with military honours. Because his family background was Chinese, the authorities had been unsure of his loyalty, and had posted him to the airport at Ho Chi Minh City to look after some captured transport planes. He had decided to defect. He had established a daily routine, taking his planes up for test flights after maintenance, with the real intention of finding out how the control tower handled incoming and outgoing aircraft, and how good their radar coverage was.

In preparation for his escape bid, he had the aircraft loaded one day with more fuel than usual, on a false pretext. He told his crew to report next day before sunrise with their US-issued certificates for C140 maintenance, and early that morning drove his family to the airport. When he announced his plan to the assembled crew and maintenance team, they all decided to join him, even without their own

A hijacked Hàng Không Việt aircraft landed at Seletar airport.

The Vietnamese aircraft successfully left the runway.

families. Everyone climbed on board. They took off and headed out over the sea maintaining a low altitude, just a few hundred feet above the water, for some distance, to avoid radar detection.

We passed him over to the US authorities, who granted him asylum.

The other hijack gave me some anxious moments. One day in 1977, late in the evening, the phone rang. An aircraft belonging to Hàng Không Việt, or Air Vietnam, was about to land at Seletar, having been diverted from Paya Lebar. It was a Douglas DC3, a small, propeller-driven airliner of a type first introduced before World War II and still in commercial service many years later. When I got to the airfield, the plane was surrounded by a police cordon.

We began negotiations with no information. We learned that the plane had been on an internal flight when hijackers struck, killing two crew and injuring a steward. After a number of exchanges, the hijackers threw down their weapons and surrendered to the police. It then emerged that they had shot the flight mechanic and the radio-operator, and had put a gun to the head of the pilot. Finding that the two shot officers were still alive, they had knifed them in cold blood. They had

flown into Thai airspace, and had been allowed to land, purely in order to refuel. The Thais had sent them on into Malaysian airspace, and they had ended up finally in Singapore. On board, beside the injured steward, there were 35 passengers, nine of them children. Negotiations went on throughout the night. We sent the injured to Toa Payoh hospital and held the four hijackers in police custody. The pilot asked for help to get the aircraft back to Vietnam with its passengers and the bodies of the two murdered crew. We arranged for refuelling and provided all the other engineering services required, hoping to have it ready to depart the following morning before sunrise, to avoid fuss and publicity.

There was a hitch.

Theoretically the runway at Seletar was not long enough for a loaded DC3 to get safely off the ground. However, next morning, the pilot decided to go for it! We had launches stationed offshore for a rescue in case he came down in the water. We had the plane pushed to the very edge of the tarmac to make the most of every inch of runway. The pilot revved up his engines furiously. I crossed my fingers, held my breath and hoped for the best. The plane roared off down the tarmac. It got off the ground just short of the airfield boundary. I breathed again.

In December 1977, the four hijackers were sentenced to the maximum penalty of 14 years in jail, plus 30 strokes of the cane. We had no desire to encourage hijacking or any other acts of terrorism.

FLYING WITH HIJACKERS

*Sometimes even civil servants must be willing to face danger, as
I discovered after terrorists hijacked a vessel in Singapore harbour.
Fortunately, the incident ended without bloodshed.*

In 1974, when I was director of the Security and Intelligence Division at the Ministry of Defence, hijackers seized the *Laju*, a small ferry owned by Shell, the oil company. By the time I reached Marine Police headquarters, the *Laju* was being shadowed by a police patrol boat. Finally it came to a halt, surrounded by police, customs and Singapore Maritime Command vessels.

The hijackers put a message in a bottle. They announced they were the 'Japanese Red Army and Popular Front for the Liberation of Palestine'. They threatened to kill their hostages unless they were allowed to leave Singapore for an 'Arab' country. At that stage we did not know who the hostages were, or how many there were.

We learned subsequently that there were four terrorists. Two of them were Japanese and two Arab. Earlier, they had set off explosive charges against four oil tanks on Pulau Bukom. They had unexpectedly been spotted, and had had to make a rapid escape. They had run to the Shell jetty, where they had hijacked the *Laju*, which was waiting to take passengers. These would have included children crossing from the island to Singapore to attend school. Fortunately, they had not actually boarded the vessel. Five crewmen were being held hostage.

Negotiations were begun, mostly by loudhailer, by Superintendent Tee Tua Bah, head of the Marine Police, stationed on his patrol boat. The terrorists asked for the Japanese Ambassador to be summoned. When we didn't respond, they sent a radio message: 'Sunset Time is Blowing Up Time.' Finally, when the ambassador appeared, and after some negotiation, they turned against him, threatening that if the Japanese police were involved, blood would flow.

That night, two of the crew escaped by jumping overboard. This gave us much valuable information on the armed status of the hijackers and the number of local hostages still on board.

Lengthy negotiations followed, involving the hijackers, the Singapore authorities, other Arab missions and the Japanese embassy. We were unwilling to fly the hijackers out on a Singaporean plane because that would only have encouraged other terrorists to see Singapore as an easy terrorist target. Proposals to fly them out on a Japanese plane came to nothing. Tense discussions lasted several days, with no solution in sight.

The sixth day brought a new development. Supporters of the terrorists had stormed the Japanese embassy in Kuwait, taking the ambassador and 15 staff hostage. They threatened to execute their hostages, starting with the Second Secretary (one of the diplomatic staff), if the Japanese government did not send a plane to Singapore to pick up the *Laju* hijackers.

The hijacked Laju *was closely monitored.*

The Japanese government finally offered to send a JAL plane. Although we did not tell the *Laju* hijackers about the embassy seizure in Kuwait, they finally agreed to be flown out to Kuwait. We insisted they give up their weapons. At last they agreed to give up their arms and explosives at the airport, before boarding the plane. They were to be accompanied by unarmed teams of Singaporean and Japanese officials.

Dr Goh Keng Swee, Defence Minister at the time, instructed me to lead the team of Singapore officials. Our mission was to hand over the Singapore hijackers to the Kuwait authorities to help resolve the situation at the Japanese embassy in Kuwait. As I said goodbye to my family, I did not mention the risks that lay ahead. We were afraid that the terrorist organisation might not let us leave Kuwait, using us as bargaining chips for the release of people in captivity in Israel or somewhere else.

As we neared our destination, I had to spell out to the authorities in Kuwait in a radio message the conditions on which we had undertaken the journey: '…13 senior officials of Singapore government must alight from the plane before the terrorists in Kuwait are taken on board. Singapore officials will leave plane and proceed straight back to Singapore. Until this is agreed and guaranteed by Kuwait government, the doors of the aircraft must necessarily remain closed. … Japanese crew and 2 senior officials will remain on board and go with the terrorists to final destination.'

When we landed, the aircraft was surrounded by tanks, armoured vehicles and soldiers carrying automatic weapons. For hours, we negotiated with the Kuwaiti authorities. I was asked to disembark from the plane and take my message in person to a Kuwaiti government minister, who was driven onto the tarmac in his limousine. Long arguments followed, involving the Kuwaitis and the Japanese ambassador to Iran, who had been brought to the scene to represent the Japanese government.

The terrorists who had stormed the Japanese embassy in Kuwait arrived at the airport – and boarded the aircraft fully armed with revolvers and hand grenades. Talking to the Japanese diplomat in Bahasa, which he understood, I persuaded him to insist that they be disarmed before the plane proceeded to its next destination. It was settled that they would keep their side arms but without the bullets – these would be kept in the hold. The Kuwaiti minister would not allow me to speak during their negotiations.

At last came the development we had all been waiting for. The Kuwaiti foreign minister arrived, and told me and my fellow Singaporeans to leave the aircraft. For several hours we were afraid that the hijackers might insist that we be returned to the aircraft as hostages, so we made ourselves scarce. However, that night we were flown safely by Kuwait Airways to Bahrain, and returned home from there on Singapore Airlines. Both groups of terrorists were flown on later to South Yemen.

The whole episode ended without bloodshed. It was good experience for me, the various ministries involved, the security service, the police and the military. While the decision to give the *Laju* hijackers safe passage out of Singapore attracted some criticism, we believed it was right. We wanted to minimise any likelihood of a terrorist group picking a quarrel with Singapore and seeking retaliation. In government you often have to make difficult decisions about serious problems with little accurate information at your disposal, and under great time pressure.

I disembarked from the plane to take my message to a waiting Kuwaiti government minister.

ENTERING THE WORLD
OF NEWSPAPERS

After a career of public service, I suddenly found myself in a completely unfamilar role: maintaining the peace between government and the media, as executive chairman of the Straits Times. *Different situations require different management approaches, as my time there demonstrated.*

I never expected to be a newspaperman. I was asked to join the *Straits Times* in October 1981, after my retirement from my civil service career.

At that time, the government was concerned about the paper's unfair coverage and negative portrayal of domestic developments without foundation. The editorial staff had asked for me to be appointed as a kind of senior mentor. They considered this the 'lesser of two evils' – the alternative might have been the imposition of a government management team, which the government was reluctant to do, unless unavoidable. In fact, I was appointed executive chairman, with powers to intervene in editorial matters if necessary.

The Prime Minister, Lee Kuan Yew, was very committed to the long-term health of the paper. The government view was that a country at Singapore's stage of development, faced with a host of social and economic challenges, could not afford a simple free-for-all, with the press taking no responsibility for the stories they ran.

Lee agreed to my appointment. He told me that he had two main concerns. Firstly, he felt that journalists were seeking to undermine government policies. Some of the younger staff were working hand-in-glove with foreign journalists, and were pursuing 'investigative journalism' western-style, presenting opinion as fact without any justification. He didn't mind if there were real skeletons in the cupboard – in that case he would be the first to ask that they be made public. But with a growing English-language readership, these little drops of venom, and

premature reporting and criticism of policies, would be disastrous for Singapore if allowed to continue. The effect would be to antagonise and distance the public from the government, and to thwart development policies designed for Singapore's growth and general benefit.

Lee Kuan Yew's second major concern was that of staff development – that we needed a core of competent local journalists with insight into the particular circumstances confronting Singapore and the problems of nation-building. They needed to bear that context in mind when discussing socio-economic policies and voicing political opinions.

The government and the *Straits Times* were on a collision course. When all this occurred, the paper was in danger of being suspended, and might have had to be completely revamped, staff and all.

One of my colleagues was Peter Lim, the paper's editor, whom I had got to know earlier during my contacts with the Singapore

Peter Lim, one of my colleagues at the Straits Times.

National Union of Journalists. He was one of those who had asked the Prime Minister for my services, and I accepted knowing that he would welcome my arrival. Most of the other staff did not greet me with open arms. Indeed, it was not until two weeks after my appointment that I was given an office in Times House, where the paper and its sister titles were edited and produced. Some of the journalists wore black armbands to mourn my arrival.

As time went on, our relationships improved. I left the management of the newsroom to the editors with no interference from me. It seemed to me that the problems at the paper were not disciplinary, but a matter of editorial management, culture and professionalism. The journalists seemed to feel that they might lose their neutral status if they were seen to support the government, however justified the government stance might be. Anything 'government' was automatically seen as suspect by young journalists. There was also a lack of balance in coverage of business and other matters. There was inadequate quality control and a reluctance to discipline staff for inaccuracies. Over time, I realised that young female journalists loved to be entertained by others, especially foreign stringers. They were often encouraged to chase rumours and treat unattributable slurs as news. The editorial culture favoured letting such stories go ahead provided the paper was not going to lose a libel case.

I also wanted to dispel the idea that I favoured letting the local press turn into a mere outlet for official statements and information. I took an interest in helping editors understand what was behind government policy. We decided to hold weekend seminars, discussion groups, for journalists from the various papers in the *Straits Times* group. Peter Lim and other senior people made presentations and critiques on such things as the writing of headlines and subheadings, and the thrust of an opinion piece. Any editor knows that these can be crafted in many different ways, and can easily be unbalanced or misleading. The talks demonstrated how published articles could have been done in a more elegant and factually correct way. The greatest number of complaints came from the business community, who were dead against any news of their company that was not favourable, no matter how accurate it was.

We made progress, but there were some dramas along the way. The fault did not always lie with the journalists. I remember a senior academic administrator

accusing the paper of a lack of balance in an article on the discontents of expatriate university staff. On investigation, it turned out that his own office had failed to provide balancing comments, despite requests.

On another occasion we were criticised abusively by a minister for publishing details of a cholera outbreak. The fact was that the health ministry had asked us to put the news out, so that local people could exercise care and prevent the disease from spreading.

There were several such incidents, often due to simple misunderstandings. My role was to act as a buffer between the journalists and editors on the one hand (who were sometimes in the wrong and sometimes in the right), and the government and civil servants on the other hand.

I was with the *Straits Times* for six years. They were not easy years, but my respect for the paper was higher when I left than when I arrived. I departed with great

Times House, Kim Seng Road.

regard for the editors, the sub-editors, the reporters, the photographers and a host of other contributors. They do not have an easy job.

One senior editor, Cheong Yip Seng, paid me this compliment: 'When we did wrong in the eyes of government, you did not just point your finger at us. You also tried to defend us and helped us learn from the experience. When we were wronged, you did not hesitate to say so to the powers that be …'

Very similar debates, I expect, are carried on even today, some 30 years later. That is inevitable in the production of a newspaper. The tensions between the media on the one hand and goverment and newsmakers on the other will always exist, and every country has to find its own way of dealing with them. I believe I helped our own journalists to do their job in a way that preserved their self-respect and was beyond reproach in the Singapore situation, without any serious compromise to their professional ideals.

I still keep up my contacts with today's editors and journalists. I spend time with them talking about problems in society today. I give them my opinion of their coverage of news in a world where newspapers are competing with television and the social media. I meet over dinner with a group of the senior editors from my time, each of us hosting in turn. That sense of camaraderie has lasted for almost 30 years.

DIPLOMACY:
THE MOVE TO MALAYSIA

After a period as a newspaperman, and looking forward again to retirement, I found myself unexpectedly returning to the world of foreign affairs, although this time as a diplomat. In general, my tour of duty as Singapore's High Commissioner to Malaysia was a pleasant experience. Many friends who were university mates and residents of the Dunearn Road Hostels were in influential positions, and were candid and even helpful in the interests of improving Malaysia/Singapore relations. At official functions people were more than generous, going out of their way to see to our comfort. However, an element of distrust developed in the government's attitude.

In April 1988, I set off for my first diplomatic posting abroad, as Singapore's High Commissioner to Malaysia. It was a challenging job. Since Separation in 1965, Singapore-Malaysia relations had sometimes been tense, as I have described earlier. Before I left, the Prime Minister told me of the high importance of the post and his interest in sorting out a number of matters then pending between our two countries, including our need for more water.

It was a new experience to be taken from the airport to the High Commissioner's Residence with a police motorcade and a Singapore flag flying on my car. The number of High Commission staff was small by today's standards, but it was, and is, a very important part of our diplomatic network. Historically, Singapore and Malaysia are closely linked. During my adult lifetime they had grown apart. My task was to help leaders and officials to get to know each other again and work together with understanding.

The differences between our countries had grown. One veteran Malay politician, Datuk Musa Hitam, observed that Singapore, being smaller and centralised, was vibrant, quick to make decisions. Malaysia sometimes showed a kampong mentality,

slow and seemingly indecisive. Malaysia is a federation, and its political set-up more complicated than Singapore. There were sometimes tensions even between federal and state authorities, between royalty and the government, between urban and rural people. He advised us to be patient in expecting results from our bilateral exchanges.

Many of the issues I had to discuss might seem familiar today. The Malaysians wanted to develop port facilities and other industries in Johor, and felt we were obstructing their efforts. There was competition between our airlines (which shared a common ancestry), and the Malaysians were worried about the effects of deregulation. They wanted to gain a larger slice of the tourism market, for Langkawi in particular. I pointed out how much Singapore had invested in attractions such as the zoo, Jurong Bird Park, the Chinese and Japanese Gardens, and Sentosa when we had no other tourist attractions to offer visitors. At one point, Singapore proposed that Singaporean motorists crossing the Causeway must have at least a half-full petrol tank. One Malaysian journalist insisted to me that our purpose was to keep Singaporeans from visiting Malaysia. I said it was simply to prevent people crossing back and forth over the congested Causeway for a cheap fill-up – but suspicions of our intentions remained.

Then there was the long dispute over land occupied by the Malayan Railway, running from Woodlands down to the railway station at Keppel Road. We wanted to get it back by negotiating acceptable terms. We were having trouble agreeing a price, and the way we should deal with some one thousand illegal squatters living on Malayan Railway land in Singapore, which was intended only to allow the trains to run. It was not until recently, in 2010, that a deal was finally reached.

There was an earlier dispute about the boundary line between Singapore and Johor in the Straits of Johor, arising from reclamation work on our side, at Tuas and Tekong. This was settled after many years when Malaysia took the issue to the International Tribunal for the Law of the Sea, which decided in Singapore's favour.

The most famous territorial argument was about the ownership of the island of Pedra Branca. This had been associated with Singapore since 1847, when a lighthouse was built on it. In 1979, Malaysia published a map that implied ownership of the island, quietly releasing it without informing Singapore. In February 1980, Singapore

registered a formal protest. Over the next few years, Royal Malaysian Marine Police boats started to make regular appearances in the waters around the island as a form of harassment. In 1989, I met the Malaysian Finance Minister, Datuk Paduka Daim Zanuddin, to give him a message from Lee Kuan Yew to Malaysia's Prime Minister, Dr Mahathir Mohamad. It expressed Singapore's concern over such developments and suggested that if the matter could not be settled between the two countries, it should be submitted jointly to the International Court of Justice. In 1994, Malaysia

The Malayan Railway station in Keppel Road.

Passions ran high during Malaysian state elections.

agreed to this course, and 14 years later, in 2008, the court ruled that sovereignty over Pedra Branca belonged to Singapore.

Among my duties as High Commissioner was to report back to Singapore my impressions of developments in Malaysia's internal politics. These were complex and sometimes stormy, with problems surrounding the judiciary and the dominant political party, UMNO. I felt I should get out of Kuala Lumpur and take the political pulse in other parts of the country. I was able to observe several federal and state by-elections, which generated heated rhetoric on all sides.

I was aware that Malay royalty was highly regarded. In slightly over a year I visited most of the states for talks with the Sultans and Governors. These were courtesy visits. We didn't get too deeply into politics, although they always had some interesting things to say. I remember very well the courteous way in which they all received me as High Commissioner. There was never any of the over-sensitivity that I sometimes met in government and political circles. My wife and I appreciated our

visits to their respective Istanas, which were furnished in a formal style without being overly ostentatious.

I believed that other officials at the High Commission should also get out and about and see what was going on in the country, taking good care to inform the authorities. I didn't want this, or my own travels, to be interpreted as espionage, given my earlier career as head of intelligence. But so sensitive were many Malaysians to the relationship with Singapore and my past, that suspicions were always there.

In 1990, Lee Kuan Yew visited Malaysia to discuss water-supply agreements between the two countries. He told me when the visit ended that Dr Mahathir had said he was unhappy with me. Mahathir thought I was too active – the insinuation being that I had been engaging in espionage. The allegation was completely without foundation. The suggestion of espionage was a puzzle to me, and it remains so. No evidence was ever forthcoming. The Prime Minister had asked Dr Mahathir for evidence, with the assurance that if it were confirmed he would discipline me. (Nothing came of this, except a note from Dr Mahathir, to the effect that the Johor authorities were unduly suspicious about my request to visit outlying areas to see economic development.)

However, I had no wish to become a problem myself, and I suggested that I be recalled. Next day, Mr Lee phoned me to say that if Dr Mahathir did not appreciate the value of having me in Kuala Lumpur, knowing that I had such direct access to my prime minister, then he was going to send me to Washington, D.C., as Singapore's ambassador.

And that is exactly what happened.

AMBASSADOR TO WASHINGTON

My appointment as Ambassador to the United States came as a complete surprise. However, operating as Singapore's eyes and ears gave me a grandstand view of developments in the world's most powerful country. I was able to study its political system, and develop a fondness for its people.

When I was appointed ambassador to the United States, I wondered how well I would do the job. But somehow, when the time came, I was able to find my way around Washington, D.C.'s web of political and diplomatic connections.

Why do we have ambassadors in these days of electronic communications? It is important that politicians and officials of foreign countries understand Singapore's domestic and foreign policies. Mistaken ideas about Singapore have to be corrected. And we ourselves have to keep in touch with what is going on in the world – because of the superpower status of the US and its global reach, we have to monitor the nature of the relationship that the US has with our neighbours and other players, such as China, India, Japan, Russia, the United Kingdom and the rest of the present-day European Union, to name a few. Important global issues are worked out in the major capitals of the world, of which Washington, D.C. is one. There is no fully effective substitute for having human eyes and ears on the spot.

I was able to watch and learn about the uniqueness of US politics at close quarters. This was a time when China was beginning to loom large in the minds of the American public. Particularly in the aftermath of the Tiananmen Square incident on 4 June 1989, the tensions with China were prominent in the media, and in the minds of human rights and other civil society groups. The Japan-bashing of the 1980s, over the growing economic success of Japan, had been replaced by China-bashing, perhaps driven partly by economic and strategic considerations. China is still the subject of heated debate in the US today.

This mood contributed to the way the US government under President Clinton

in his first term approached its role in maintaining world peace, and particularly its response to Iraq's invasion of Kuwait in late 1990. I was at an embassy staff event when Operation Desert Storm was launched in January 1991. The attack was broadcast live on CNN. I think the whole of Washington was watching. In March, Iraq accepted a ceasefire, and the United States and its coalition partners declared victory. I attended a victory parade, over which 'stealth' bombers flew for the first time in public. Singapore's flag was displayed during the parade.

I regularly took part in think-tank gatherings at the time. They were a useful opportunity to learn from analysis and discussion of international relations, and defence and strategic issues. The general opinion, following Operation Desert Storm, was that technology had reinforced US military superiority. There was confidence that the US had shown the world that its security commitments should not be taken lightly. At the time the American public was looking for a 'peace dividend', following the end of the Cold War and the recent demise of the Soviet Union, expecting that defence budgets could be cut, and that American troops would only have to fight in one, or maybe one-and-a-half, theatres of conflict. Defence experts believed that the US would be able to rely on 'expeditionary' forces that could be deployed briefly in trouble spots at short notice. How wrong they were, as events in the next decade would prove.

I witnessed several campaigns leading up to presidential and congressional elections. In Singapore we have a Westminster-style, first-past-the-post electoral system. American elections are very different. At the beginning of my term, I found the system confusing. The process is very long-drawn-out. Candidates spend much time and energy on fund-raising. Tremendous funds are spent on electioneering and TV advertising of various kinds.

It took me some time to understand the concept of 'primaries', held by the Republican and Democratic parties before their national conventions, at which they nominate their presidential and vice-presidential candidates. I learned that the conduct of primaries varies from state to state. For instance, in some states an elector's vote is treated as just an expression of opinion about a candidate, which the party in the state is not obliged to follow. There are other differences too.

To take 1992 as an instance, media commentators expected the New Hampshire primaries to have a big impact on the presidential nominations. The Democratic candidates included Bill Clinton, then governor of Arkansas – but when the results were announced it was Senator Paul Tsongas who had come out on top. The pundits were proved wrong in this case. For the Republicans, the incumbent President George H. W. Bush (father of President George W. Bush) was in the lead, followed by the aggressively right-wing Pat Buchanan.

In common with other heads of diplomatic missions, I was invited through the State Department to the opening session of the Democratic Party Convention at Madison Square Garden, New York, in July 1992. The venue is famous for hosting world championship boxing matches and basketball tournaments. We diplomats were seated high up in the hall – the people sitting down at ground level and the speakers on the stage looked Lilliputian. The acoustics were terrible. In fact the proceedings were not easy to follow, drowned out by the din of incoming state delegations and supporters entering the stadium from all directions, with accompanying bands. When Bill Clinton's nomination as presidential candidate was announced, confetti and balloons showered down from the ceiling.

The most memorable part of the Republican Party Convention in August that year was a speech by former resident, Ronald Reagan. As one of my diplomatic colleagues noted at the time, 'Using his wit, self-deprecating humour, and husky, seductive voice, Reagan seemed to cast a spell over the convention.' I personally attended the last two days of the event, and it was sadly obvious that the speech of President George Bush made less of an impact on the audience than that of the old charmer Reagan. And indeed, Bush went on to lose the election to Clinton. During the campaign he showed signs of fatigue, and it was said that he was even thinking of dropping out.

On 20 January 1993, Bill Clinton was sworn in as the 42nd President of the United States on the steps of the Capitol Building. With the other ambassadors, I took my place near the podium and had a clear view. It was a bitterly cold, wintry day, with signs of frost on the ground. We felt the full blast of the wind coming down Pennsylvania Avenue. Although I was warmly wrapped up in overcoat, hat

and muffler, I was glad of the blankets provided to cover our legs. Afterwards, the long walk back to our parked cars restored my blood circulation.

What did I learn from my time in the US? I left Washington with great fondness for ordinary Americans – friendly, hospitable and polite. I was surprised by the continuing importance of religion in the lives of many people. I was impressed by the freedom of debate in the media, even though some of it is drowned out by crass vulgarity. I appreciated the liveliness of a 'constitutional' society, where people argue endlessly, as opposed to an 'adherent' society, where what the leader says goes without question. Americans have no fear of speaking out, often loudly. We Asians think that opening our mouths risks causing offence. Both sides are in danger of being misjudged as a consequence.

I left the US with one firm view about the access that diplomats can expect from the American establishment. During the 'Michael Fay' incident I was, in effect, *persona non grata* so far as government agencies and the White House were concerned. A small country, even with the closest of relations with the US, generally does not count. Your country has to be a 'great opportunity' or a 'serious problem' if you are to get attention.

VANDALISM AND THE CONVICTION OF MICHAEL FAY

While I was ambassador to the US, a case of vandalism in Singapore developed into a serious bilateral dispute. Following the conviction of a young American in Singapore, I had to make it clear to the American public that Singapore has its own laws and judicial system, and that Americans in Singapore, like anyone else, should respect them.

In 1993, Singapore experienced a serious outbreak of vandalism, involving cars. At least 67 vehicles were affected. One of the youths responsible was Michael Fay, a young American, who was convicted in March 1994 of vandalism, mischief and dishonestly retaining stolen property. Fay was sentenced to four months' jail, six strokes of the cane and a fine. He was punished together with several others from various countries in the region.

Caning, which the Americans view as 'flogging', is controversial, depending on people's sympathies. At a time of rising crime in the US, some Americans supported the punishment. Others didn't. I was worried that our actions might be projected as inhumane by the American media. An American newspaper stirred up its readers with a graphic account of caning that had been published earlier in Singapore deliberately to frighten hardcore criminals and secret society gangsters. A few of the press reports in the US were simply false.

An article appeared in the *New York Times* inviting the public to protest by phone to our embassy in Washington, D.C. We set up an automatic answering system. A recorded message told callers who opposed the punishment to 'press 1' and those in favour to 'press 2'. (Those in favour outnumbered those against.) One message read: 'Please listen very carefully. This is the American Vigilance Committee. If Michael Fay is harmed in any manner whatsoever by the Government of Singapore, a citizen of Singapore presently within the boundary of the United States of America will be executed. This is the only warning you will receive.'

I was given security protection by the US Secret Service.

President Bill Clinton prematurely criticised the punishment, even before making a formal appeal, so arousing public opposition even more. He later sent a formal message to Singapore's then president, Ong Teng Cheong, supporting a plea for clemency that had been lodged by Fay's parents. Clinton, to be fair, stressed his respect for the competence of the Singapore legal system. However, he appealed for the caning sentence to be commuted, in view of Fay's youth, the fact that he was a first offender and his personal circumstances. In response to this appeal, Fay's punishment was reduced from six cane strokes to four.

It was my job to pass this news to the White House. We hoped that the Americans would appreciate the reduction, but it was not enough for them. They did not accept that we could not practise double standards, one set for Americans and another for locals. We caned some of our own criminals for serious offences, as we did offenders from neighbouring countries. Singaporeans, and the governments of countries nearby, were watching closely to see if an American would get special treatment.

Shortly after Fay's conviction, I was asked to appear on the TV talk show, 'Larry King Live'. Prepared for a public grilling in front of a worldwide audience, I kept my cool under pressure and stated Singapore's case. Fay's father, also on the show, was kept in a separate room – according to a programme representative, there were fears he might assault me on-camera! I am pleased to say that the public response was generally good. The punishment went ahead, and Fay served his prison term.

In June 1994, Fay returned to Los Angeles, accompanied by his mother. I was concerned that his arrival might become a big media

Michael Fay and one of the vandalised cars.

I appeared on the 'Larry King Live' talk show, expecting to be grilled.

event, stirring up further controversy at Singapore's expense. However, on that day, another sensational event exploded all over the TV networks. The police were chasing American football star O.J. Simpson down a Los Angeles highway, intent on arresting him for the alleged murder of his ex-wife Nicole Brown and her friend Ronald Lyle Goldman three days earlier. Helicopter-mounted cameras were following the chase, which was attracting nearly 100 million viewers. This drama continued for several days. Nothing came out of the TV coverage that was expected on Fay's return to the US.

That was the end of the Michael Fay episode. With time, the adverse reactions died away.

However, there was a minor student demonstration the following year, when Prime Minister Goh Chok Tong was visiting his alma mater, Williams College, in Boston. Goh seized the opportunity to restate Singapore's position. His message was that Singapore is a small and vulnerable country, very different from the United States. Americans should not expect Singapore to be like the United States. As Prime Minister he was responsible for governing Singapore the way Singaporeans wanted. During the protest, one man chained himself to the pillar of the entrance to the hall, where Prime Minister Goh was to be honoured. The police kept an eye on him, until the early hours of the morning, when the demonstrator, unable to bear the cold, begged them to break his chain and have him returned to the bus terminal. That was the extent of his commitment to protest.

THE PRESIDENCY

Sometimes life can take you completely by surprise, even when you think you may no longer be useful. Several times in my career, fate has thrown up completely unexpected challenges, none greater than the one presented to me at the age of 72. I had just returned to Singapore from the United States, and was all set to coast gently into retirement.

One night, at around 11.00 pm, the phone rang. At the other end of the line was Senior Minister Lee Kuan Yew. He asked me to go and see him the following day. 'Hey presto,' said my wife. 'Another great challenge. Perhaps we are going to be uprooted again.'

Lee told me that the government was preparing to nominate a suitable candidate for the elected presidency, and asked me if I would stand. I was taken totally by surprise. Later, my wife said, 'How can you say "No"?'

Over the years, whenever I have been called on to do anything for the country, I have never turned away from duty. The support of my family and friends, and especially that of Lee Kuan Yew, eventually persuaded me to shoulder the special duties of the presidency.

I was not sure how my candidacy would be received by the general public. Unlike most Singaporeans, I am not ethnically Chinese. My close association with Lee Kuan Yew, and my stint as intelligence chief, might have put a few people off.

In the event, I was elected unopposed. No eligible alternative candidates presented themselves. I was sworn in on 1 September 1999. I was the second president of Singapore to be elected; the first was Ong Teng Cheong. (His predecessor, Wee Kim Wee, was deemed 'elected' during his term, following a change to the constitution.)

People often assume that the president has the power to do what he likes. In reality, the president's position is largely symbolic. He (one day it might be 'she') is head of state, not head of government. He is not an executive president, like the President of the United States.

One of the president's duties is to deliver the speech at the Opening of Parliament on behalf of the government, setting out its forthcoming programme of legislation. Although the president does not write it, I always saw an early draft and made comments. Sometimes I suggested a change of emphasis, or asked for passages to be rewritten, so that they could be read out in a more natural way, or to avoid a phrase being misunderstood or too vague.

The role of the president is symbolic. People expect him to be a check on the government. In general, according to the constitution, that is not his role. He must always act in accordance with the advice of the Cabinet. He can send advice back for reconsideration, if he has sound reasons. Ultimately, if the advice remains unchanged, he is duty-bound to act on it. However, he has a power of veto in a number of key

At the Opening of Parliament, I delivered a speech on behalf of the government.

areas, especially in regard to the use of the nation's reserves – financial and in the form of land – as well as key appointments in government. This he must use in consultation with the Council of Presidential Advisors.

In addition to the powers laid down by the constitution, the president has, by custom the right to be consulted, the right to warn and the right to encourage. The way he exercises these customary rights depends on the relationship he has with the Prime Minister and the elected government. Sometimes it is helpful for the president to act as a sounding board for the prime minister, to share problems and to give a perspective on solutions the government may have in mind. A president can ask for advice from the cabinet to be reviewed. He has access to all the information that goes through the cabinet system – it is good that it should be open to scrutiny by another pair of eyes.

The president has to respond to appeals for clemency made on behalf of people sentenced to death in the courts of law. It is a painful thing to sign a death warrant. However capital punishment takes place only after a long process of review and appeal. I followed the progress of every clemency request as it came up in the cabinet papers. If I had some doubts – say, if the evidence seemed circumstantial and unconvincing – then I asked the attorney-general or the solicitor-general for a briefing. I always took the trouble to make sure that everything had been done according to the law to ensure justice was done.

In 1991, when the elected presidency was introduced through amendments to the constitution, some additional powers were given to it. The president was empowered to approve certain key appointments in the public service. Most famously, he was given the power to prevent any future government from irresponsibly spending financial reserves built up by previous governments. This power is sometimes called the 'second key' to the reserves. During my first term, I had to use that key, as I will explain in the next story.

During my first term of office I sought re-election. Again there was no candidate standing against me. I was elected unopposed in August 2005. Some academics claimed that, as there was no contest, I could not be considered properly elected. This criticism came to nothing and I successfully completed my second term in 2011.

THE SECOND KEY

*As I explained in the previous story, under changes to the
constitution that were made in 1991, the elected president controls
a 'second key' to Singapore's national reserves, i.e. finances and
land belonging to the government.*

The elected president's role, so far as the reserves are concerned, takes the form of a 'veto'. This is a Latin word meaning, literally, 'I forbid'. In this context, it means the power to forbid an irresponsible government to fritter away reserves built up by its predecessors. The key word here is 'irresponsible'. The possibility of calling on the reserves arose several times during my time as president.

Singapore depends on exports for its prosperity. In 2001, demand for our goods, particularly electronics, took a dive all around the world. The recession that was threatening many countries worldwide also hit our economy. The government considered the necessity of drawing on past reserves. They hoped that the recession would be temporary. They were later proved right. The following year, growth was back on track. The 'second key' was not used.

In 2002, there was another proposal to use the 'second key', this time to allow redevelopment of some older HDB housing estates. For en-bloc redevelopment, the government had to buy flats back from their owners at a fair price. The plan was to fund these purchases with money borrowed from the reserves, and return it to the reserves afterwards, using the proceeds from vacant land resold profitably after the redevelopment. Initially I was not happy with the idea, because there was no guarantee that the land would indeed be sold at a good enough price. The Ministry of Finance came up with a more stringent way of measuring the likely profitability of such deals, and on that basis I gave my approval, with the agreement of the Council of Presidential Advisors.

The year 2008 brought a more severe test of the second key system. In the last six months of that year, the economy took a sharp downward turn. The origin of

this setback was a sharp drop in house prices in the US. A property 'bubble' had developed there. Many people were buying homes at inflated prices using mortgages they could not afford, in the mistaken belief that property values would always go on rising. Suddenly, it became obvious that American banks had been lending money that they might never get back. In September, Lehman Brothers, a leading American investment bank, went under, with debts of over US$600 billion. Other financial institutions too came under great pressure.

The US was facing a full-blown financial crisis. All companies need credit, whether for long-term investment or for day-to-day transactions. Without it, the world's economy would come to a halt. American banks were cutting back on lending, which affected American business generally. There were serious side-effects in Europe and Japan. No part of today's global economy is insulated from the rest. The Singapore government noted the exceptional efforts of foreign governments to stimulate their own economies, and were considering what measures might be necessary at home in Singapore.

Towards the end of 2008, the situation was developing fast. Around the world, several countries announced that depositors would be protected if a bank were to go under. Although our banks were strong, the government decided to give a similar guarantee, subject to an overall upper limit, so that our banks would not be put at a disadvantage. This might require the use of reserves, and I gave my agreement. Around the same time, in October, the Prime Minister told parliament that the government was preparing measures to help businesses and households cope with the recession. He did not, at that stage, foresee the need to draw on past reserves for this.

By November, the situation was worsening. The Prime Minister announced that the budget for 2009 would be brought forward to January, and outlined several new measures, including a loan access scheme for businesses and a training programme for workers, to help those who had been retrenched acquire new skills and be ready for the new jobs that were expected to come after the recession.

As we moved into 2009, the crisis deepened still further. With the US economy deteriorating and the entire global financial system in jeopardy, the crisis was unlike anything Singapore had faced since independence. This was the situation that finally

led the government to ask the President's agreement that it should to draw on past reserves. Uppermost in their minds was the need to save jobs. My office raised concerns about tapping past reserves when current reserves were still available. The Ministry of Finance explained that they wanted to retain some current reserves in case anything more unexpected happened, which was quite likely with the global economy in such a state of near-crisis.

In mid-January the Prime Minister came to me and explained that the money would be used for an innovative 'jobs credit scheme', as well as for a risk-sharing scheme to make access to credit easier for businesses. Under the jobs credit scheme the government paid a subsidy to employers for all jobs they provided. This was very effective in preventing retrenchments, and helped companies get going again when conditions improved.

I gave the go-ahead for the use of past reserves for this 'resilience package', as it was called. Some members of the public questioned the decision. On 17 February, I gave an interview to the press explaining the reasons behind it. Looking back, I am sure that the Council of Presidential Advisors and I took the right decision, and I am glad we did it quickly. Any delay would have allowed the economic situation to become even worse than it was and hinder our ability to recover.

The amount actually drawn from the past reserves for the resilience package was S$4 billion. In February 2011, the government paid it back to the reserves in full, although it had no legal or constitutional obligation to do so. As to the scheme for guaranteeing bank deposits, it expired on 31 December 2010, without being used. Just having it in place had generated the confidence that was needed.

A PRESIDENT PAYS US A VISIT

As head of state, the President of Singapore represents the nation when foreign heads of state visit Singapore in their official capacity. These visits are formal occasions, follow a set pattern, and require detailed preparation. During my tenure I received several heads of state on state visits.

L et's take one state visit as an example. In March 2011, His Excellency Viktor Yanukovych, President of the Ukraine, visited Singapore. As is customary, the ceremonial welcome took place at the Istana, our seat of government. It followed a well-established and well-rehearsed sequence, with every step choreographed in advance.

First, I arrived at the Istana and took the salute of a contingent of the Singapore armed forces. Then, at the main porch, I awaited the arrival of the Ukrainian

The President of the Ukraine received a ceremonial welcome.

President. As he mounted the saluting dais, the guard-of-honour presented arms, both national anthems were played, and the flag of the Ukraine was unfurled. The visiting president then inspected the guard-of-honour. He signed the visitors' book, and was welcomed by a line of Singapore dignatories, including members of the cabinet, and members of the diplomatic corps (representatives of foreign countries in Singapore).

After that came the 'official call', for which the Ukrainian President and I sat in armchairs flanked on each side by delegations from the two countries. The photographers got their shots, and then we had a conversation, through interpreters. Such exchanges are short, and often rather formal, and they are not expected to be used to raise matters that either side is concerned about, or to set the agenda for the more detailed discussions that officials carry on later. That is reserved for the government – the Prime Minister and his cabinet. On this occasion, the Ukrainian President then went on receive a courtesy call by our Prime Minister.

In the evening I hosted a state banquet. At pre-dinner drinks our chief of protocol presented a group of our own ministers and other important guests to President Yanukovych, and I was introduced to members of their delegation. Towards the end of dinner, both presidents made a speech. Among other topics, I compared Singapore's position at the gateway of China, India and Southeast Asia with Ukraine's strategic location in Europe. I welcomed developing ties in the fields of academia, research, science and technology. President Yanukovych paid tribute to Singapore's achievements, of particular interest as the Ukrainians were trying to bring many aspects of their own national life up to international standards.

The preparations for a state banquet are elaborate. Tables have to be set up, floral arrangements created, silverware cleaned. Under the leadership of the Istana's head of household, the staff must run over the whole proceedings in advance, taking into account the planned sequence of events, the correct way to serve guests and the demands of diplomatic protocol. Menu planning can be a challenge, and the people at the Ministry of Foreign Affairs often advise on cultural and dietary requirements. The Istana has its own kitchens, although generally on such occasions the food is prepared by one of Singapore's top hotel chefs.

The visiting president and I engaged in a conversation through interpreters.

Spouses have an important part to play. My wife has always found it quite easy to get on with the wives (or husbands) of visiting heads of state. During courtesy calls or banquets, she was almost always able to strike up a relaxed conversation. Originally we served visitors conventional tea, but later we offered them 'longan tea'. It was a particular hit with the Empress of Japan. People liked it, and it gave them something to talk about, breaking the ice.

One thing I learned was how to carry on a conversation through an interpreter. There is no point in trying to make jokes – they lose their point very easily in translation. It is important not only to be interested in what you are talking about, but also to show it, as a glum or weary moment can very easily be caught by a newspaperman's camera.

REPRESENTING SINGAPORE AS HEAD OF STATE OVERSEAS

My two terms as president were punctuated by regular state visits abroad, as representative of the nation of Singapore. My job on these occasions was to create goodwill, and an overall framework for the more detailed work of ministers, civil servants, business representatives and others. I made state visits to all ASEAN countries except Myanmar, and to other Asian countries including China, Japan, South Korea and India.

Preparing the programme for a state visit starts months ahead, when the host country asks what the visitor would like to see. A month or so before I set off, an aide-de-camp would make a reconnaissance trip, accompanied by someone from the Ministry of Foreign Affairs and one of the security team, who would liaise with their foreign counterparts.

Before departing, I would receive a small, pocket-sized programme detailing the schedule day-by-day. State visits involve ceremonies, and even the lower-profile parts of the programme can be quite formal. If both sides know what to expect, there is less likelihood of embarrassment or unintentional offence. State visits, inward and outward, should run like clockwork.

To give a flavour of these visits, I will describe one I made in 2010, to Finland, accompanied by a delegation made up of officials and members of parliament. Landing in Helsinki after a flight from London, we emerged from the airport into weather conditions very different from the hot and humid Singapore we had left behind. On the drive to Helsinki and the Hotel Kamp, where we were to stay, we saw sweeping, wooded landscapes. Most of the trees were shedding their leaves, while some retained a yellowish glow. It was late autumn, chilly but exhilarating.

The arrival ceremony was quite simple. We were received by President Tarja Halonen and her spouse, Pentti Arajärvi, a university academic. After the two national anthems, I met the Finnish delegation-of-honour and inspected the guard-

of-honour. This was followed by a conversation during which I introduced my son Osith and granddaughter Monisha, who were accompanying us. Then came a meeting between the two delegations, at which both presidents discussed political issues.

Lunch was hosted by the mayor of Helsinki in the City Hall, only 200 metres away. My host, the Finnish President, suggested we walk there, which we did, arm in arm. At the lunch, I was presented with the Medal of Honour of Helsinki, which I accepted on behalf of the people of Singapore.

I was received by President Tarja Halonen in Helsinki, Finland.

Later that day, accompanied by our delegation, I took part in a wreath-laying ceremony at the tomb of the Unknown Soldier, representing all those who had perished in the defence of their country. A second wreath was laid in memory of Field Marshal Mannerheim, who led Finland in its battle against the invading Russian army just before the start of World War II in Europe in 1939. The atmosphere in the cemetery, surrounded by woodland, was solemn and dignified.

The state banquet that evening was unusual, in that we were greeted by a line-up of kitchen staff, waiters and butlers, a reflection of Finland's egalitarian society.

The programme for the following day included a meeting with Mari Kiviniemi, the Prime Minister (both the president and the prime minster were female). Then followed a trip to the headquarters of Nokia, the maker of mobile phones, where a number of Singaporeans were working. Later, we visited Neste Oil, who were planning to open a €500-million plant in Singapore later that year. In the afternoon

President Tarja gave a state banquet during my visit.

the Foreign Minister, Alexander Stubb, briefed us on the evolution of the European Union's foreign policy.

On the third day, I met the speaker of Finland's parliament. The three MPs in the Singapore delegation were able to discuss a programme of exchange visits by parliamentarians from the two countries.

We then moved on to Turku, about 150 kilometres from Helsinki. There, on behalf of the people of Singapore, I accepted the Medal of Honour of Turku. The day ended with a visit to the cathedral there, mother church of the Evangelical Lutheran Church of Finland, and the country's national shrine. It has borne witness to many of the most important events in the nation's history – the sound of its bells is broadcast at noon on national radio.

No two state visits are exactly the same. Visiting South Africa, Namibia or Botswana, as I did in mid-2007, was a very different experience from visiting Japan in 2009. Australia in 2005 was very different from Turkey four years later. But the underlying purpose is always to foster cooperation and goodwill in a range of fields, including commerce, science and technology, academia, defence, security and others. Visits to shrines, war memorials or other places of symbolic importance are not empty ceremonies. They generate goodwill, and help establish a backdrop against which other forms of communication can take place and relationships flourish.

PRESIDENT ON PARADE

After I became president, one of my duties was to act as reviewing officer in the National Day Parade, when the nation celebrates its national identity. Although I was a little nervous at first, I managed to do my bit without making mistakes. I enjoyed the celebratory mood, and felt at one with the public.

National Day is one of the most important events in the Singapore calendar. It falls on 9 August, to commemorate the day in 1965 when Singapore became an independent sovereign nation. The highlight is the National Day Parade, which brings all Singaporeans together. The real, multiracial Singapore is on parade. Most foreign visitors watching the event admire this national get-together.

I stopped to talk to individual personnel during my inspection of the parade.

Each year, people of all races and ages are full of patriotic enthusiasm, enjoying each part of the programme. Singapore is on display, and this generates a kind of euphoria. Everybody cheers the arrival of the Prime Minister, the arrival of the presidential motorcade and the parade itself. When I was president, the setting was the National Stadium. This great structure was completed in 1973, in time for the 7th Southeast Asian Peninsular Games. It was a wonderful venue. The acoustics of the arena added to the intense atmosphere of any big event.

Before I became president, I had absolutely no idea that one day I was going to be part of that parade. But by the time the first National Day of my presidency came along, in the year 2000, I knew what I had to do. For a moment, when the motorcade took me into the arena, I felt uncertain. How should I greet the crowd? Do I turn left, turn right or what? Slowly the car made its way round the parade ground. As it did so, I relaxed. I soaked up the atmosphere and then everything came naturally.

One of my tasks was to review the parade. Rather than just walking along the ranks of uniformed personnel and saying nothing, I stopped and talked to a few individual soldiers. Usually one was selected from each of Singapore's main racial groups, and different contingents from the armed forces and the police. Of course we didn't want them to be completely tongue-tied, and so they were given advance warning. I could identify the ones to talk to by means of a little mark on the ground. I tried to get them to relax, asking them perhaps about their run-out date, or what they were going to do later as a career. Sometimes, I had a word with a female member of the police or the navy.

While all this was going on, the crowd were probably wondering what on earth we were talking about. But conversations of this kind remove any sense that the people on parade are being taken for granted. I enjoyed them as much as the individuals concerned, who were pleased to be seen talking to me in front of the huge crowd.

When it was all over, I sometimes went down and talked to some children or other members of the crowd. This was far more than a public-relations gesture. They had been selected to recite the National Pledge at the end of the event. The least I could do was to show appreciation for their efforts.

The high point of National Day comes when the crowd sings the national anthem, 'Majulah Singapura'. More than once I was asked why, as president, I did not join in. It was certainly not because I didn't know the words! The answer is simple. By singing the anthem members of the audience are renewing their pledge to Singapore. The president stands there as a symbol of the whole nation, not as one of the spectators.

Once the celebrations are over, and we have all gone home, preparation for the next year's event begin. The Ministry of Defence is in charge of everything, including the entertainment. This is a time when military expertise in planning and logistics shows its value. Every year brings something different, designed to be more appealing to the crowd.

The National Day parade. The president is a symbol of the state.

The president also has to take part in the annual passing-out parade of the Singapore Armed Forces. The ritual is slightly more complicated. It involves handing over the ceremonial sword to the winner, and witnessing religious leaders saying their prayers, observing a moment of silence for those who have passed away, changing the colours and handing over the colours. I didn't have a chance to rehearse, having to make do with a briefing by my *aide-de-camp*. Fortunately, I made the right moves at the right time.

You can never predict the weather in Singapore accurately. But nature was always kind to me. Only once do I remember it starting to rain heavily during a passing-out parade. There was some kind of covering overhead, but I felt that as those on parade were going to get wet, it was not fair to expect anything different for myself. So I got wet too.

RECOGNISING ACHIEVEMENT

It is very important for the president to keep in touch with the community. This is one reason I valued the National Day Awards ceremony, which recognises exceptional achievements by individuals.

The list of award recipients comes out on National Day, 9 August, but the presentation takes place in November. In the later years of my presidency, the venue was the University Cultural Centre at the National University of Singapore.

The presentation event takes a lot of organisation, involving as many as 50–60 *aides-de-camp* on the day, all displaying their guest-management skills. Up to 500 people may be there to receive their awards. For each of them, the moment is very memorable. I tried as far as possible to have a word with each of them, addressing them by name, and thanking or congratulating them. If a person was handicapped, I moved away from my normal location to greet them, even if this was a break from protocol. Sometimes, these chats held up the proceedings, but I felt they were worth doing – this is a rare moment for the recipient and for his or her family, who are often present. The handshakes went on for two hours or so, and you had to concentrate hard, so that the process didn't become mechanical, and therefore meaningless. All the award-winners had their photos taken – I tried to get them to relax. After the ceremony I would mingle with them and their families, having a chat and giving them photo opportunities. I always enjoyed informal contact of this kind. This is a moment when the president comes down from his high pedestal and is one of the crowd.

The presidency must be close to the people, giving a sense that the country has some permanent institutions other than the government. This had nothing to do with me personally – individual presidents, like individual politicians, come and go. It is the presidency as an insitution that should be permanent. This is why I feel the President's Awards are very important. There are awards connected to the Scouts, Guides, Boys' Brigade, teachers, nurses, social services, design, environment,

science and technology, and school soccer. There is an Exemplary Mother award, and my own name is attached to a soccer challenge trophy for polytechnics and other tertiary institutions. Most of these awards are presented in the Istana at different times of the year.

The nature of presidential patronage changed during my presidential terms, and this was deliberate. At the outset, it did not go far beyond social gatherings in aid of good causes. Over time, my involvement became deeper and more wide-ranging. I supported over 30 organisations as patron-in-chief or patron; and I was appointed Chief Scout!

In my official role as president, I attended over a thousand events held to foster a huge range of socially useful activities. The range of things that people do in Singapore is amazing. They include sport and leisure, volunteerism, the professions, youth organisations, arts and heritage organisations, the sciences, technology, tourism and other areas of commerce, education, the uniformed services, philanthropy, religious and other traditional festivals, trade unions, the handicapped and otherwise disadvantaged, and much more besides.

I regarded building such connections as an important part of the president's job. But there is a wider significance. Non-governmental activities are becoming an increasingly important feature of Singapore society, and they give individuals a way of making a personal contribution outside their main employment. I hope every young Singaporean reading this book will try to play a part in them.

The National Day Award ceremony is a big event for the award recipients.

HELPING THE LESS FORTUNATE

Some people need a helping hand from society.
When I became president, I wondered what part I could play.
This led to the creation of the President's Challenge, a yearly campaign
consisting of events and activities that raise funds for charity.

I have never forgotten the hardships I endured as a child; nor the difficulties I saw ordinary working people facing when I was involved in social and trade union work. Through my social studies course at university I saw the importance of charitable work. In 1960, I became honorary general secretary of the Council of Social Service, as it was then called, and I was greatly influenced by the man who headed it for over 30 years. This was Dr Ee Peng Liang, who spent a lifetime helping Singapore's less fortunate in many ways, and was widely known by his nickname, 'Mr Charity'.

My predecessors as president, from President Yusof Ishak onwards, played a high-profile role in promoting voluntary welfare activities. They acted as patron of many associations and supported fund-raising efforts through events such as concerts and gala dinners. I decided I wanted to continue these activities, but also reach out more broadly to the community, getting people from all walks of life involved in helping others.

This is why, in the year 2000, I started the President's Challenge and continued to support it throughout my time as president. Also involved were the National Council of Social Service (NCSS) and the Ministry of Community Development. As Singapore has become more prosperous, our social problems may have changed, but they have not disappeared. We still have to look after the blind or people with particular physical or mental disabilities; but there are broader needs too. There are new problems associated with a modern, flourishing society, such as family or child abuse and juvenile delinquency. Rehabilitation of drug users and those who have been jailed, making prisoners productive even inside prison – these are all new areas that cry out for our help.

The President's Star Charity is a programme designed to help the under-privileged.

The Challenge was my personal call to Singaporeans of all ages and from all walks of life to strengthen our spirit of community caring and volunteerism. I wanted individuals, corporations and voluntary and religious organisations to work with the government in creating a society in which 'Every Singaporean Matters'. It is important that the less well-off have a sense of hope, and feel that someone does care for them. In some cases, we looked overseas to see what other countries had done to tackle similar problems.

We set out to persuade people that every contribution matters – even a single dollar. And to a large extent, I think we were successful. In this way, volunteer service was seen as valuable. Participation in President's Challenge events has grown steadily over the years. In the first 11 years we raised some $100 million. The Singapore Totalisator Board and Singapore Pools were sponsors, helping run the Challenge without charging for their efforts, and so we could distribute the funds in full.

On one occasion I had to perform on the President's Star Charity Show, a television programme organised every year by MediaCorp to raise funds for the President's Challenge. I am not much of a singer – reciting a poem seemed a safer choice! 'Desiderata' by Max Ehrmann is about happiness. I chose the section on 'hope'. I practised the passage over and over again. It felt like being back at school! But the end result was worth the effort, and I was touched by the generosity of those who called in during the show to pledge donations.

WORKING WITH LEE KUAN YEW

*As a young civil servant I found myself in regular contact with
the Prime Minister and other senior leaders. I got a sense of their vision
for Singapore, observed their way of working, and gained knowledge
and experience that laid the foundation of my future career.*

I first saw Lee Kuan Yew and his wife, Kwa Geok Choo, in the audience at political
debates and forums at the University of Malaya. He did not take an active
part, but always seemed very attentive, looking around him at the audience,
working out who was who, taking stock. When I was Secretary of the University
Socialist Club, I heard talk among the more radical committee members of their
meetings with Lee at the Medical Students' Hostel in Paterson Road. According to
these accounts, he was deeply involved in their 'struggle', to the extent that I even
wondered if he was a communist sympathiser.

My view changed when I was working in the civil service as a Seamen's
Welfare Officer, and heard through colleagues of Lee's private revelations at the
Political Study Centre of serious differences with extreme left-wing or communist
sympathisers within the PAP and the cabinet, and his call to senior civil servants to
rally behind him and the government in his mission to seek independence. During
the election campaigns prior to self-government, his rally speeches showed him
to be the kind of leader that I felt Singapore needed. He fired my imagination and
gave me a sense of mission in serving Singapore.

I first met him face to face when I was working with the Labour Research Unit,
although most of his dealings were with Devan Nair. He must have known through
Devan what I was doing. In early 1964, I was instructed to represent Singapore at a
meeting of the Afro-Asian People's Solidarity Organization in Algiers, and negotiate
Singapore's acceptance as a member. I went to Sri Temasek to be briefed, and there
found Dr Goh Keng Swee and Lee Kuan Yew sitting on the porch. Goh gave me
my instructions. Lee did not contribute, preferring to practise his golf swings on

the nearby green. This trip was important to my career. With only a basic brief, I successfully represented Singapore in a political tussle that was very different from routine civil service administration, and I think this may have led our leaders to see my potential.

When I first joined the Ministry of Foreign Affairs (MFA), I was essentially a note-taker, doing what I was told. I attended meetings between the Prime Minister and visiting leaders and foreign heads of diplomatic missions accredited to Singapore. My task was to make a record of the conversation. I learned how to capture the essence of the exchanges and the way our leaders got their messages across. We were a small team at MFA, working with very little experience in diplomacy or security.

The leaders often had to take decisions on the basis of inadequate evidence, but they were prepared to take risks if they felt the arguments were sound. Under stress they could have their moods, and in my dealings with them at those times I learned to tread with care. Lee displayed extraordinary energy. He read widely on world affairs and economics, and even when he was impatient, one was always aware of the depth of his thinking. The strength of his convictions always showed, as did his determination to achieve his aims.

Initially, I was very low in the MFA hierarchy. But after Lee got to know my work he used to call me directly and ask me to do things. This would upset the permanent secretaries, who resented this disregard for the line of command. But Lee was never a stickler for protocol – he would cut through it just to get a job done. One of his achievements in the early days was to get the civil service on his side, but he had no time for anyone who was excessively bureaucratic.

This was a tense but exhilarating time for a rookie like me, and taught me more than any college or textbook could have. Because we were a young and small organisation, not yet set in our ways, it was possible for young officers such as myself to get noticed and enjoy prospects for promotion that we might not have had in today's larger and more professionalised civil service.

Lee was always very systematic in the way he worked – his desk was always clear except for the one file he was working on. He never wasted words. His instructions were brief – even cryptic at times. There was very little familiarity or small talk.

As our working relationship developed over time, I had a sense that he felt I would understand what he wanted. He was an excellent writer and expected the same of others. He expected notes of meetings to be concise, no more than four pages, double-spaced. At MFA my first direct working contact with him arose when I was asked at short notice to take notes for a meeting he was having with the visiting Thai foreign minister. I grabbed a necktie, put on a jacket and rushed to the meeting. On my arrival at the door, Lee came towards me. In a paternal way he smiled, straightened my tie and said, 'You must remember you are no longer in the labour movement.' I cherish that memory to this day. My note of that meeting was done from memory, immediately afterwards. It was well received. My next one was based on copious and detailed notes, and did not go down so well. Lee called me up and said, 'Do you think I have the time to read all this?' Despite the pressures, he was not bad-tempered, although he could be impatient, and I did occasionally witness a tongue-lashing given to someone else – thankfully I escaped that experience.

Lee's mind was at work 24 hours a day. If he travelled anywhere, he was always asking if something he saw could be applied in Singapore. He would grill anyone he met for ideas that could be useful – many a time I saw foreign dignatories or other experts emerge from a meeting with him in a state of exhaustion, after he had pumped them for ideas and information. He very rarely had a purely social conversation. He was intensely focused, all the time.

Because I felt instinctively in tune with Lee's political aims, I found it easy to work with him. When he decided to accept separation and the creation of a totally independent Singapore in 1965, he showed great statesmanship. During my subsequent career in the public service, which lasted over half a century, I never had any reason to change my high opinion of the man who, more than any other individual, created modern Singapore. I feel privileged to have worked with him.

INDEX